THE

REAL DIRT

ON AMERICA'S FRONTIER LEGENDS

THE
REAL DIRT
ON AMERICA'S FRONTIER LEGENDS

JIM MOTAVALLI

GIBBS SMITH
TO ENRICH AND INSPIRE HUMANKIND

For my wife and daughters, who indulge and support my writing.

First Edition
23 22 21 20 19   5 4 3 2 1

Published by
Gibbs Smith
P.O. Box 667
Layton, Utah 84041

1.800.835.4993 orders
www.gibbs-smith.com

Cover designed by Nicole LaRue
Interior design by Devin Watson and Virginia Snow
Printed and bound in Hong Kong
Gibbs Smith books are printed on paper produced from sustainable PEFC-certified forest/controlled wood source. Learn more at www.pefc.org.

Library of Congress Cataloging-in-Publication Data
Names: Motavalli, Jim, author.
Title: The real dirt on America's frontier legends /
   Jim Motavalli.
Description: First edition. | Layton, Utah : Gibbs Smith, [2019] | Includes
   bibliographical references and index.
Identifiers: LCCN 2019000231 | ISBN 9781423652601 (hardcover)
Subjects: LCSH: West (U.S.)--Biography. | Explorers--West (U.S.)--
Biography.
   | Frontier and pioneer life--West (U.S.) | LCGFT: Biographies. | Legends.
Classification: LCC F590.5 .M68 2019 | DDC 910.92/2 [B] --dc23
LC record available at https://lccn.loc.gov/2019000231

Title page photo: Buffalo Bill with Sitting Bull, who appeared regularly in his Wild West shows. (Library of Congress)

CONTENTS

PREFACE

WE WERE MISINFORMED: MYTHS IN AMERICA'S FRONTIER LORE

The American frontier pushed continuously west from the 1630s to the 1880s, at the same time it was also moving both north (into Maine) and south (all the way to Florida). But it was the westward imperative that caught the public's imagination. In his historic speech at the 1893 World's Columbian Exposition in Chicago, historian Frederick Jackson Turner expounded his "frontier thesis," which held that "the existence of an area of free land, its continuous recession, and the advance of American settlement westward explain American development."

But for the western frontier to get settled, there had to be advance scouts, explorers who—sometimes inadvertently—made the wilderness "safe for civilization." These mountain pioneers, trappers, and traders—extant after 1810—were a motley crew indeed, and often far from heroic.

True mountain men were never numerous—maybe there were three thousand of them, according to the 1980 *Marriage and Settlement Patterns of Rocky Mountain Trappers and Traders.* Only half were Anglo-Americans, from such places as Kentucky, Virginia, the Louisiana Territory, and points east. A quarter were either French-Canadian or French-American. The rest were African-American, Spanish-American, Native Americans, or Métis (mixed ancestry, Native American and European-American).

Their era didn't last long—the insatiable lust for furs, unmediated by anything resembling a conservation plan, meant that the great natural resources (and beavers in particular) were largely played out by the 1840s. But because the public couldn't get enough frontier tales, no matter how tall, many of these colorful figures were enshrined in legend as true American pioneers.

If trapping wasn't as lucrative as before, the mountain men found they could get work as guides, scouts, and Indian fighters. And then there were new opportunities—on stage.

No less a figure than legendary P. T. Barnum had an early hand in creating the legend of the American West. According to Michael Wallis's *The Real Wild West*, it was in 1843 that Barnum encountered a herd of fifteen buffalo near Boston and promptly bought them for seven hundred dollars, later staging "The Great Buffalo Hunt," complete with lariats wielded by pretend Indians.

Some twenty-four thousand people went to see the animals in Hoboken, New Jersey (admission was free, but Barnum had chartered the ferries from New York and pocketed the thirteen-cent roundtrip fee), and many fled in terror when the herd of buffalo broke through a fence and then took shelter in a nearby swamp. Plenty of other people came to a later Wild West show that Barnum staged. When a party of Indians visited President Abraham Lincoln in 1864, Barnum waylaid them to attract paying customers to his New York museum. Introducing an unsuspecting Yellow Bear, the chief of the Kiowas, Barnum described him as "probably the meanest, black-hearted rascal that lives in the Far West."

We think we know a lot about Lewis and Clark, Davy Crockett, Daniel Boone, Jim Bridger, Hugh Glass, Jeremiah Johnson (whose actual name was John "Liver-Eating" Johnston), "Nature Man" Joe Knowles, William "Buffalo Bill" Cody, and their like, but in fact much of what we think we know is a mishmash from sensationalized newspapers, dime novels and old penny dreadfuls (usually written by ghostwriters who never left their city offices), Wild West shows, highly speculative third-hand accounts, and Disney movies from the

P.T. Barnum somewhere between 1860 and 1864. He got in early on the Wild West flim-flam. (Charles D. Fredricks & Co./Library of Congress photo)

coonskin cap days. Fact and fiction have intermingled in a fairly alarming way.

How popular were dime novels in their day (1860 to about 1900)? Very. New York–based Beadle & Company published its first short book, *Malaeska: The Indian Wife of the White Hunter*, in 1860, and its *Seth Jones; or, The Captives of the Frontier* (written by a twenty-year-old schoolteacher who lived most of his life in New Jersey) sold five hundred thousand copies.

By 1864, according to the *North American Review*, Beadle had more than five million novels in circulation—incredible in those days of a less-literate, less-populous America. But the company was dead by 1896.

Dime novels made a star out of Edward Z. C. Judson, who wrote under the pen name Ned Buntline, and the real people he wrote about became famous. He met William Frederick Cody out west, and made him a household name with his much-reprinted 1869 *Buffalo Bill, the King of the Border Men*.

"Exaggeration was part of the natural idiom of the West," reports *American Heritage*. "No boast was too big, no tall tale too outrageous. Men declaimed ridiculous

Edward Z. C. Judson, who wrote under the pen name Ned Buntline, churned out dime novels by the dozens. (Sarony photo/Wikipedia)

Teddy Roosevelt took natural history seriously, despite his determination to eliminate large swaths of it, and he went after the "Nature Fakers." (Wikipedia photo)

brags that ran on to considerable length: they were ring-tailed roarers, half-horse, half-alligator; they were sired by a hurricane and rode the lightning, and on and on."

Further, the frontiersmen were products of their times, which generally saw nature as a cornucopian bounty without cease. The Pilgrims landed in a pristine wilderness but (after deforested England) found it dark and forbidding. The concept of stewardship or living in harmony with nature is mostly applied to these people in an act of revisionist wish fulfillment.

And as Teddy Roosevelt famously observed in his 1907 "Nature Fakers" essay in *Everybody's Magazine*, much of what passed for wilderness lore and animal behavior studies in the nineteenth and early twentieth century was sentimental, anthropomorphic claptrap. "The modern 'nature faker' is of course an object of derision to every scientist worthy of the name, to every real lover of the wilderness, to every true hunter or nature lover. But it is evident that he completely deceives many good people who are wholly ignorant of wild life," Roosevelt wrote. He was particularly aghast at a story that described a humanitarian wolf leading home some lost children, "in a spirit of thoughtful kindness."

Roosevelt had in mind such wildly popular authors as Ernest Thomson Seton (*Wild Animals I Have Known*, 1898) and William J. Long (*School of the Woods*, 1902). The naturalist John Burroughs had earlier gone after Long and his ilk in a 1903 *Atlantic* magazine essay entitled "Real and Sham Natural History." Burroughs responded to Seton's claim that his stories were true. "True as romance," he said, "true in their artistic effects, true in their power to entertain the young reader, they certainly are but true as natural history they as certainly are not."

It's interesting to note that an aggrieved Long fired back at Burroughs's "astounding criticism" later that year in the *North American Review*, claiming that, through patient study, he'd actually *seen* animals committing the wondrous acts he described, and he double-checked by talking to guides and trappers. "Nearly every one of them has at least three or four animal stories that would not be believed if they were printed," Long wrote. "The truth is that they have discovered unconsciously the secret of animal individuality, which the old natural history writers have missed."

Long went on to describe two orioles building a nest with skills that would require a graduate degree in architecture, and affirmed that foxes do indeed go for rides on sheep's backs.

Of course, there was plenty of silly stuff around besides the work of sentimental nature writers, including the tall western tales (often presented as autobiography) that publishers were turning out in droves. If it carried a gun and roamed the wilderness, it was grist for the reading public. Come to think of it, given fanciful films like *The Revenant*, it's still true today. The movie posits an Indian wife and son for trapper Hugh Glass, making reality of what at best was a rumor.

The truth is that much of the folksy lore we've inherited from these homespun pioneers is probably wrong, and the history we have mostly leaves out the women and minority groups who were also very much part of the scene.

In fact, there's a long-running battle between traditional western historians—who held on to a heroic view—and the revisionists, who maintain that the old guard's writing often ignores the major roles played by women, African-Americans, Asians, and Latin Americans. Or as *The New York Times* put it, "In their view, white English-speaking Americans did not so much settle the West as conquer it."

In the corrected record the West is, according to the *Times*, "a land in which bravery and success coexist with oppression, greed and failure; in which decaying ghost towns, bleak Indian reservations, impoverished barrios and ecologically devastated landscapes are as characteristic of western development as great ranches, rich farms and prosperous cities."

Views like this have drawn potshots from such popular figures as the novelist Larry McMurtry, who refers to the new history as "failure studies" that "rarely do justice to the quality of imagination that constitutes part of the truth."

Revisionism has made inroads, and it's sometimes reflected in modern western movies and literature. But the popular myths remain powerful. McMurtry, who can see both sides of an argument, wrote in the autobiographical *Walter Benjamin at the Dairy Queen*, "Readers don't want to know and can't be made to see how difficult and destructive life in the Old West really was. Lies about the West are more important to them than truths, which is why the popularity of the pulpers—Louis L'Amour particularly—has never dimmed."

Let's consider the figure of "Wild Bill" Hickok, whose legend was considerably bigger than the actual (in his later years) rather dispiriting figure. The early Hickok was dashing enough, with his

"Wild Bill" Hickok definitely started out well, but the later years were all anticlimax. (Wikipedia photo)

long hair and waxed mustache, and he did keep law and order in Kansas as sheriff of Hays City and marshal of Abilene. "His ironhanded rule helped to tame two of the most lawless towns on the frontier," reports Biography.com.

The few real notches on Hickok's gun (one of them being his own deputy, shot by mistake) was inflated to one hundred by the time the yellow press was done with him. The legend was abetted by the lawman's appearances in Buffalo Bill's 1873 melodrama *The Scouts of the Plains.* There, the legendary lawman did not distinguish himself as a thespian. According to *The West:*

"He had a high girlish voice that was hard to hear, and whenever the spotlight failed to follow him closely enough, he would step out of character and threaten to shoot the stagehands. Buffalo Bill finally had to let him go when he could not be dissuaded from firing blank cartridges at the bare legs of the actors playing Indians, just to see them hop."

In later years Hickok suffered from glaucoma and lived on his fame as a gunfighter, posing for tourists, gambling, getting drunk and arrested for vagrancy. He was shot in the back of the head during a card game in Deadwood, South Dakota, in 1876, holding what became the "dead man's hand"—aces and eights.

The Cheyenne Daily Leader struggled to reconcile the legend with the actual man they had known. "Seven or eight years ago his name was prominent in the … border press, and if we could believe the half of what was written concerning his daring deeds, he must certainly have been one of the bravest and most scrupulous characters of those lawless times," the newspaper said. "Contact with the man, however, dispelled all these illusions, and of late, Wild Bill seems to have been a very tame and worthless loafer."

These revelations didn't hurt Wild Bill's legacy; he was even a legend in his own time, which is why (as we shall see) both Calamity Jane and Buffalo Bill exaggerated their roles in his life. In what Woody Allen called the Radio Days, Wild Bill's story was turned into a rootin' tootin' shootin' 1951 serial—with Andy Devine as pal Jingles, and Kellogg's Corn Pops ("that great new cereal with the sweetener already on it") as a sponsor. Hickok had become "the greatest fighter of them all," and "always on the side of law and order." No vagrancy for the clean-cut actor Guy Madison, who portrayed the gunfighter as a straight shooter. His horse's name was Buckshot.

The Adventures of Wild Bill Hickok was also on TV with the same cast from 1951 through 1958—when kids couldn't get enough westerns. Much later, Keith Carradine portrayed Hickok in the contemporary HBO series *Deadwood*, named after the very town where the great man was shot to death. In the actual town of Deadwood today, you can see the murder acted out every summer day, and it's also commemorated in wax. Wild Bill's "death chair" is in a glass case.

In recent years, helped by the Internet and the new availability of old texts and documents that had previously languished in libraries, we're able to cast fresh light on our ancestors—and not all of it is flattering. In fact, most of it isn't. Did Davy Crockett really die fighting in the Alamo? It's a bedrock part of Texas history, but it may not have happened.

This book, then, is a corrective, a look not only at the lives these larger-than-life figures led, but also at the examples they set. Were the mountain men farsighted explorers and savvy stewards of the wilderness they inhabited, or ruthless exploiters of it? The truth is they were a bit of both, and see if you don't agree with me after reading these historical portraits.

In choosing who to profile in *The Real Dirt on America's Frontier Legends*, I've selected both household names and lesser-known frontier figures. I've included an African-American wilderness guide, a Spanish mountain man who received the first license to trade furs with the Pawnee, and a black woman who passed as a man to serve as a Buffalo Soldier. Together, they give us a fuller picture of how the frontier was, if not won, at least subdued. Don't expect heroics. The buckskin will be looking a bit frayed by the end of the book.

In some ways, *The Real Dirt on America's Frontier Legends* is a sequel to my 2008 book *Naked in the Woods*, a biography of the great "Nature Man," Joseph Knowles, who doffed his clothes and spent two months in the wild and wooly woods of Maine. You'll meet Knowles here, too, and come to have some doubts about what he did or didn't do with all those trees for cover.

Like many of those profiled, Knowles was a great storyteller, and truth was a moving target for him.

Dodge City, Kansas Peace Commissioners, left to right, Chas Bassett, W. H. Harris, Wyatt Earp, Luke Short, L. McLean, Bat Masterson, Neal Brown. (Camillus S. Fly photo/ # 111-SC-94129, National Archives)

DANIEL BOONE

A LEGEND
IS BORN

(IN PENNSYLVANIA)

DANIEL BOONE

Daniel Boone became a legend after the publication of a—somewhat fanciful—1784 biography. (Alamy Stock)

THE LEGEND

Born to Quaker parents near Reading, Pennsylvania in 1734, "Dan'l" Boone had little use for the classroom, instead finding his education in the woods. He was, as the History Channel puts it, "a scrappy lad who loved hunting, the wilderness and independence." Boone, whose stint as a farmer was mercifully short lived, was always looking for the frontier—and finding it, too. Famously, he wanted more "elbow room." He went first with his parents to the wilds of northwest North Carolina, then lived mostly in his beloved "Kentuck"—as wagoner, explorer, and pioneer (leading the way through the Cumberland Gap), settler (Boonesboro is named after him), Indian fighter (he even spent time as a prisoner of the Shawnees), and politician—as a state legislator.

Like Davy Crockett, he was a moral and upright man who couldn't take civilized constraints for long, but was always off again to new adventures, new places to hunt, and new territories to discover.

HOW THEY GET IT WRONG

Boone's immortality can in part be attributed to one John Filson, author of the 1784 *Discovery, Settlement and Present State of Kentucke*, which contains a whole first-person appendix on "The Adventures of Col. Daniel Boon."

Read today, "The Adventures" clearly reflect their times. Filson did interview Boone, but the flowery language is his alone. "Thus we behold Kentucky," Boone supposedly said,

> lately an howling wilderness, the habitation of savages and wild beasts, become a fruitful field; this region, so favorably distinguished by nature, now become the habitation of civilization, at a period unparalleled in history, in the midst of a raging war, and under all the disadvantages of emigration to a country so remote from the inhabited parts of the continent.

Filson's book sold well in both America and Europe, ensuring that Boone was a frontier legend in his own time.

More than most wilderness explorers, Boone appears to have had a genuine love and enthusiasm for nature. Boone, with embellishments added by Filson, exclaimed on his perilous existence in Kentucky in 1770, surrounded by dangers, both human and animal,

> The prowling wolves diverted my nocturnal hours with perpetual howlings; and the various species of animals in this vast forest, in the day time, were continually in my view. Thus I was surrounded with plenty in the midst of want. I was happy in the midst of dangers and inconveniencies. In such a diversity it was impossible I should be disposed to melancholy. No populous city, with all the varieties of commerce and stately structures, could afford so much pleasure to my mind, as the beauties of nature I found here. . . . The diversity and beauties of nature I met with, in this charming season, expelled every gloomy and vexatious thought.

Left as a kind of wilderness Thoreau, this version of Boone might have been something close to the truth, but instead he comes down to us today mostly as an Indian fighter and an action hero—almost indistinguishable from Davy Crockett (without the death at the Alamo; he died of natural causes in Missouri).

Michael Wallis's *The Real Wild West* describes Boone as "America's first cowboy," since he spent part of his childhood in Pennsylvania tending cattle. Wallis writes, "Exaggerated accounts of Boone's exploits, especially at Cumberland Gap and on the new Wilderness Road that ran north through the fertile bluegrass countryside, inspired

three future American heroes—Davy Crockett, Kit Carson . . . and William F. 'Buffalo Bill' Cody."

Boone's adventures also inspired James Fenimore Cooper, and even Lord Byron wrote about "The Colonel Boon, back-woodsman of Kentucky." Byron's 1823 poem, a eulogy, added that Boone was happiest going after his bears and bucks, and in such pursuits he "enjoyed the lonely, vigorous, harmless days of his old age, in wilds of deepest maze."

Of course, it gets less literary than that. Typical is a 1950s comic book called *Exploits of Daniel Boone*, which depicts him in full buckskins and coonskin cap, having gun-totin' adventures with his sidekick, the similarly clad Sam Esty. This version of Boone is also displaying some of the real man's legendary honesty. In one panel, he tells a group of Indians, "Most of you know me! We've fought, but fought honorable. No man can say Dan'l Boone ever lied to him or broke a promise!"

This rough-and-tumble image is contradicted by Laura Abbott Buck's 1872 *Daniel Boone: Pioneer of Kentucky*, which notes,

> Many suppose that he was a rough, coarse backwoodsman, almost as
> savage as the bears he pursued in the chase, or the Indians whose terrors
> he so perseveringly braved. Instead of this he was one of the most mild and
> unboastful of men; feminine as a woman in his tastes and his deportment,
> never uttering a coarse word, never allowing himself in a rude action. He
> was truly one of nature's gentle men.

Boone certainly dispatched Native Americans during his lifetime, but on balance he was not unsympathetic to their plight. In later years, when asked how many Indians he'd killed, he replied, according to *Daniel Boone: The Life and Legend of an American Pioneer* by John Mack Faragher, "I am very sorry to say that I ever killed any, for they have always been kinder to me than the whites."

As Buck paints the relationship, "The Indians seem to have had great respect for Boone. Even with them he had acquired the reputation of being a just and humane

"Daniel Boone Protects His Family," an early print that shows his legend as an Indian fighter building. (Library of Congress photo)

man, while his extraordinary abilities, both as a hunter and a warrior, had won their admiration." This portrait, written one hundred years after the events, informs the view we have today.

Boone's 1823 biography reinforces this view, opining that he was

> a great friend to the Indians, notwithstanding that they had been his mortal enemies in the early part of his life—it was frequently remarked by him that while he could never with safety repose confidence in a Yankee he was never deceived by an Indian . . . [He] should certainly prefer a state of nature to a state of civilization, if he was obliged to be confined to one or the other.

In his own words, at least as they come down to us through not entirely reliable sources, Boone said that describing Indians as "undisciplined savages" was "a capital mistake, as they have all the essentials of discipline."

George Caleb Bingham (American, 1811–1879), "Daniel Boone Escorting Settlers through the Cumberland Gap, 1851–52." Oil on canvas, 36 1/2 x 50 1/4. (Mildred Lane Kemper Art Museum, Washington University in St. Louis. Gift of Nathaniel Phillips, 1890.)

WHAT WE ACTUALLY KNOW

Daniel Boone fits his legend better than most wilderness pioneers. He really did have a love of nature, and he sought out wild places. He was the first explorer in eastern Kentucky in 1769, and despite many troubles there returned in 1773. He's credited with building the Wilderness Road through the territory (taken by, among many others, Abraham Lincoln's grandfather), pioneering the Cumberland Gap as a way in, and helping build the forts that made Kentucky habitable by settlers. He was a great hunter, and at least until the 1880s a beech tree grew near Boone's Creek, Tennessee, with the legend, "D. Boon killed a bar. 1775."

Daniel Boone's reputation as an honorable man remains intact.
(Library of Congress photo)

In the days before mountain men, Boone was known as a "Long Hunter," because he'd be gone from his home in North Carolina on lengthy rambles in search of deerskins (which could fetch fifty cents each). In 1769, Boone met up with an old friend, John Finley, who got him excited about the rich opportunities for hunters in the new territory of Kentucky. The pair followed an old Cherokee trace Finley knew about, and it took them through the narrow Cumberland Gap and into the glorious prairies and forests of what became Kentucky's bluegrass country.

Boone and Finley spent two years in the wilderness with a constantly changing cast of characters. It wasn't an easy trip—Boone's brother-in-law was killed, and all the hard-won hides they'd collected were stolen by Cherokees. But they'd seen a wonderful and cultivatable land with huge pigeon roosts, vast flocks of fat wild turkeys, bears, deer, elk, and buffalo.

Despite opposition from both the government and the resident Cherokees, Boone led a group of settlers back to Kentucky in 1773. Tragedy struck again, when Boone's eldest son was killed by Indians near the Cumberland Gap. The survivors retreated, but in 1775 Boone was again sent into Kentucky to cut a trail through the Gap to the Kentucky River. Soon he and his fellow adventurers were building cabins in the new town of Boonesborough. Kentucky settlement grew rapidly.

All of this depended on agreements with the Shawnee and Cherokees that were, of course, frequently broken in later years.

DANIEL BOONE, POLITICIAN

Both Daniel Boone and Davy Crockett spent time as politicians, but Boone's time as a legislator is less well known. He was first elected to the Virginia legislature in 1781, elected again in 1787, then a third time in 1791. He also served as both sheriff and county lieutenant of Fayette County, Virginia, around this time.

Legislators led adventurous lives back then. In 1782, the by-then Colonel Boone fought Indians in the Battle of Blue Licks, which resulted in an ambush that killed his son, Israel. During his legislative term he was also captured for several days—and held in a coal house—as part of a broader British kidnapping plot that was to also have included Thomas Jefferson (who was then governor of Virginia).

Boone represented several different constituencies in the legislature, including, after being elected in 1787, Bourbon County (which he described as a hunter's paradise). Legislating was very part-time when Boone lived in Maysville. The area was mostly small farms, so the issues weren't exactly weighty matters of state. Maysville was a bustling place, and Boone did well there, keeping a tavern, surveying, and speculating in land and horses. He owned seven slaves at that time. His later years were less secure.

Boone was too restless to remain a politician for long, and maybe he didn't like all the backroom deals he saw going on. It's interesting to note that in 2003 a controversy arose when the Daniel Boone Parkway in the Kentucky he'd helped settle was renamed for Congressman Hal Rogers—who'd brought in the federal funding. "I'm humbled," Rogers said, but many of his constituents were outraged.

"I think we're getting a little carried away naming things after politicians," said Kentucky educator Mike Mullins. But, of course, Boone was also a politician in his day.

Boone acquired a great deal of property in the newly pacified territory, but like Davy Crockett he was a terrible businessman and ended up losing all of it. "He made and lost large amounts of money speculating in Kentucke land, buying and selling vast tracts," reports Bill O'Reilly's *Legends and Lies: The Real West*. "His common decency was his greatest business flaw, as he was too often reluctant to enforce a claim to the detriment of others."

Bedeviling Boone his whole life was a 1780 robbery that relieved him of twenty thousand dollars (an enormous sum at the time) worth of scrip and land certificates that had been entrusted to him by settlers. It took him thirty years to repay them, which he did mainly by selling off his land. He was reportedly left with fifty cents after making the last payment.

In 1799 he left Kentucky for Missouri, settling in the wild Femme Osage valley, dying there twenty-five years later. In his eighty-first year, he was still going out on long hunting trips up the Missouri to the Yellowstone. On the other hand, Filson's 1823 *The Life and Adventures of Colonel Boon* relates that around that same time, when he was no longer able to pursue wild animals with his usual dexterity, he would track his bears to a hollow tree, "and by means of smoke would drive them therefrom, and shoot them as they retreated." It doesn't sound all that sporting.

Boone died in 1820, with the final words, "My time has come."

There's only one portrait of Daniel Boone that was painted from life. He's not wearing a coonskin cap, but looks like a sharp-featured gentleman of his time. Paintings of a young Boone in fringed buckskin are of more recent origins.

There's plenty of "fake news," but Boone really did love hunting, the outdoor life, and a wilderness to explore. (Library of Congress photo)

IN THE FOOTSTEPS OF DANIEL BOONE

Because he lived so long ago, and never saw the Wild West, the actual Daniel Boone is perhaps one of our more shadowy frontiersmen. But you can walk in his footsteps today, thanks to some well-conceived memorials.

Boone's birthplace in Birdsboro, Pennsylvania, is known as the **Daniel Boone Homestead**, operated by the Pennsylvania Historical and Museum Commission. The recreated home built by Boone's parents, Squire and Sarah, is impressive, and uses the construction methods then in vogue.

At the **Cumberland Gap National Historical Park**, you can see where Boone helped build the Wilderness Road and open Kentucky to settlement in 1775. An added bonus is that you can see where three states—ol' Kaintuck, Tennessee, and Virginia—come together.

Would-be outdoorsmen and women who want to blaze a trail can explore the **Daniel Boone National Forest** in Kentucky. A special management area honors hunting with what are known as "pioneer weapons"—crossbows and muzzle-loaders (aka flintlocks) are allowed but breach loaders, not so much.

Don't forget **Fort Boonesborough State Park**, near Richmond, where you can see the recreated fort that Boone and his team built. It's a working site, with cabins, blockhouses, and period furnishings.

Boone moved to North Carolina in 1750, and lived there twenty years. In that state, there's the **Daniel Boone North Carolina Heritage Trail**, with an interactive map to act as guide. Drop in on **Boone**, the town named after this great American pioneer. A play about Boone, *Horn in the West*, is staged in the town every summer. If you travel the Blue Ridge Parkway, there's an exhibit at mile marker 285 for Daniel Boone's Trace, which is where he left a marker for his route to Kentucky.

Daniel Boone's memorial in Louisville, Kentucky. The statue is by Louisville-born sculptor Enid Yandell. (Library of Congress photo)

WHAT HE SAID

Boone may have wanted elbow room, but—at least in his purported writings—he sure liked the idea of taming nature (and its native inhabitants) for Christianity. He wrote,

> Here, where the hand of violence shed the blood of the innocent; where the horrid yells of savages, and the groans of the distressed, founded in our ears, we now hear the praises and adorations of our Creator; where wretched wigwams stood, the miserable abodes of savages, we behold the foundations of cities laid, that, in all probability, will rival the glory of the greatest upon earth; and we view Kentucky, situated on the fertile banks of the great Ohio, rising from obscurity to shine with splendor, equal to any other of the stars of the American hemisphere.

He returned to this theme of a wild land civilized late in his life.

> Two darling sons, and a brother I have lost by savage hands, which have also taken 40 valuable horses, and an abundance of cattle. Many dark and sleepless nights have I been a companion for owls, separated from the cheerful society of men, scorched by the summer's sun, and pinched by the winter's cold, an instrument ordained to settle the wilderness. But now the scene is changed: peace crowns the sylvan shade.

Boone also famously said, "I have never been lost, but I will admit to being confused for several weeks."

DAVY CROCKETT

NOT EVEN

BORN ON A MOUNTAINTOP

DAVY CROCKETT

The larger-than-life Davy Crockett, with trademark dog and gun. Artist John Gadsby Chapman actually met Crockett in the 1830s, but painted this full-length portrait after the Alamo made him famous. (Alamy Stock)

THE LEGEND

Growing up in a mountain wilderness, young David Crockett was killing bears before he was out of short pants (the first one at age three). This "ring-tailed roarer" became a skilled hunter, trapper, scout (fiddle player, too), and fought Indians but learned their lore (and was respected for his honesty by them). Like Daniel Boone, he left civilization behind when it started to close in on him. When his friends Sam Houston and Jim Bowie were in trouble in Texas, Crockett and his trusty rifle, "Betsy," headed west to fight with them for freedom. He died fighting for liberty, taking many Mexicans with him, and finally swinging old Betsy when he ran out of bullets.

HOW THEY
GET IT WRONG

The popular image of Davy Crockett, in breezy biographies (of which there are dozens), highly imaginative Hollywood films, and even his own autobiography, tend to skip over the stiff-looking politician in a city suit (he served as both a state representative and as a not very successful congressman) that survives in contemporary paintings and gives us a noble (if bloodthirsty) wilderness warrior whose word was his bond. Sure, he was a backwoods politician, but a politician nonetheless—and he might have stayed one if the voters were willing.

The legend also vastly oversimplifies the history of Texas, turning it into a liberty-or-death freedom struggle, rather than a complex, controversial, and somewhat dubious land claim.

The fanciful Crockett Almanac *of 1836. (Library of Congress photo)*

WHAT WE ACTUALLY KNOW

To quote from John Ford's *The Man Who Shot Liberty Valance*, "When the legend becomes fact, print the legend." That appears to be particularly true in the case of Davy Crockett. "Born on a mountaintop in Tennessee/Greenest state in the land of the free/Raised in the woods so's he knew every tree/Killed him a bear when he was only three." So goes the song from the Disney TV show that every boy knew in the 1950s. But in fact, Crockett was born in the Tennessee lowlands, and—despite actor Fess Parker turning it into a fad—there's only sketchy evidence that he ever wore a coonskin cap. He preferred to be called David Crockett, not Davy, and only headed for Texas—and his appointment with destiny—after failing as a politician.

Crockett may have been a crack shot and the terror of the raccoon and ursine population, but he always struggled to be a provider. As he described it, "I found I was better at increasing my family than my fortune." After his first wife died, leaving him in humble circumstances with three children, he "married up" to a well-to-do widow, Elizabeth Patton, with a two-hundred-acre farm.

Luckily, Crockett found his calling in public life. After moving west to Lawrence County, Tennessee, in 1817, he was elected as a magistrate, then, in 1821—thanks to the generous provision of applejack and corn liquor to the voting public—as a state legislator. He became known as "the gentleman from the cane," which was meant as an insult, but Crockett embraced the backwoods image.

Crockett could charm his constituency, but he was no businessman. As Robert Morgan writes in the book *Lions of the West: Heroes and Villains of the Western Expansion*, he was frequently "cheated, taken advantage of, overtaken by bad luck," and victimized by bad weather or acts of God. Let's examine the career of Davy Crockett, Mississippi River trader.

The Disney film *Davy Crockett and the River Pirates* (1956) is a TV series compilation starring Fess Parker (who played Daniel Boone, too) and Buddy Ebsen. In it, Crockett

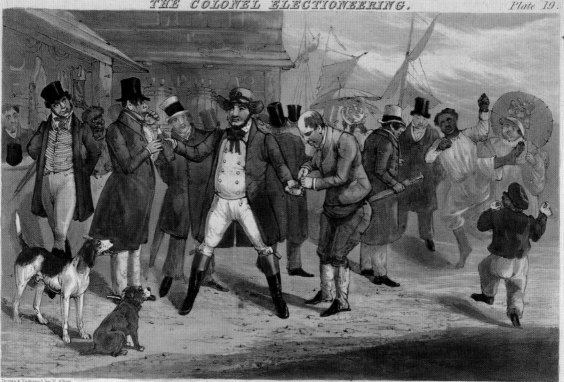

Drawn & Engraved by H. Aiken.   LONDON: PUBLISHED AT 51, ELY PLACE. E.C.

HOW TO GET A VOTE, *OR GOING FIXED FOR THE PURPOSE.*

B. "Where did you spring from, Colonel?" Col. "O! I've just crept out from the cane, to see what discoveries I could make among the whites .... you think you have greatly the advantage of me. B. 'tis true I live forty miles from any settlement; I am very poor, and you are very rich; you see it takes two 'coon skins here to buy a quart, but I've good dogs, and my little boys at home will go their death to support my election, they are mighty industrious; they hunt every night till twelve o'clock; but it keeps the little fellows mighty busy to keep me in whiskey. When they gets tired, I takes my rifle and goes out and kills a wolf, for which the state pays me three dollars, so one way or other I keeps knocking along." B. "Well, Colonel, I see you can beat me Electioneering." Col. "My dear fellow, you dont call this Electioneering, do you? When you see me Electioneering I goes fixed for the purpose. I've got a suit of deer leather clothes, with two big pockets, so I puts a bottle of whiskey in one, and a twist of tobacco in t'other, and starts out: then if I meets a friend, why I pulls out my bottle and gives him a drink:— he'll be mighty apt, before he drinks, to throw away his tobacco, so when he's done, I pulls my twist out of t'other pocket and gives him a chaw: I never likes to leave a man worse off than when I found him. If I had given him a drink, and he had lost his tobacco, he would not have made much; but give him tobacco and a drink too, and you are mighty apt **TO GET HIS VOTE.**" Son of David Crockett.

and his sidekick, Georgie (Ebsen), need to move their trapped furs downriver to the market in New Orleans, and encounter the legendary keelboatman Mike Fink— whom they rather improbably beat in a slapstick race. It all ends happily, with the cargo offloaded in New Orleans.

In reality, after being defeated in a race for Congress in 1825, Crockett did indeed decide to try his hand at the river trade. He hired a crew to make thirty thousand

Davy Crockett, electioneering. He excelled at it, but didn't always win. (Library of Congress photo)

Crockett in rustic garb, as painted by William Henry Huddle in 1889. (Wikipedia)

barrel staves—then in great demand. Crockett took it upon himself to provide the crew with meat. At *that*, he excelled, soon killing, butchering, and salting enough bear meat to last for months. He was less successful at building and operating flatboats.

The very first day out, Crockett's crew lost control of their boats, which crashed into some floating trees and broke apart. The whole cargo was lost near Memphis, and the men were lucky to be rescued after clinging to their surviving boat for a very cold night. Fortunately, in celebrating his rescue in a tavern with a group of admirers, Crockett favorably impressed a new benefactor, Marcus Winchester, who bankrolled a new—and successful—bid for Congress.

Crockett entertained thoughts of the presidency, but he made many enemies with his opposition to Democrat Andrew Jackson's policies—including the president's Indian Removal Act, relocating Native peoples who lived east of the Mississippi. Still, he managed to stay in office (with a gap between 1831 and 1833) until 1835. Crockett told a crowd in Memphis after his defeat, "Since you have chosen to elect a man with a timber toe to succeed me [victor Adam Huntsman had a wooden leg], you may all go to hell, and I will go to Texas."

And go to Texas—and perish there at the Alamo—is exactly what he did. Defender Jim Bowie probably did not invent the Bowie knife (his brother Rezin did), but he is popularly and likely inaccurately depicted on film as rising from his sickbed to use that blade to deadly effect on his Mexican enemies.

That colorful account of Bowie's end appears in the 1848 *Col. Crockett's Exploits and Adventures in Texas*, supposedly consisting of Crockett's "found" diary. Its authenticity has been questioned, to put it mildly. "[T]he dying Bowie, nerving himself for a last blow, plunged his knife into the heart of his foe, who were scaling the wall," Crockett supposedly had time to jot down.

And Colonel William Travis probably never drew the much-celebrated "line in the sand" at the Alamo with his sword. What's more, Crockett may well have survived the climactic battle at the Alamo.

Davy Crockett, legislator. He ran afoul of Andrew Jackson, who he called a "greater tyrant than Cromwell, Caesar or Bonaparte." (Image number 1/102-107, Courtesy of Texas State Library and Archives Commission)

An epic fight it wasn't. Phillip Thomas Tucker writes in *Exodus from the Alamo: The Anatomy of the Last Stand Myth,* "More of a rout and a slaughter than a battle in the traditional sense, the struggle for the Alamo lasted only about twenty minutes, making it one of the shortest armed clashes in American military history for an iconic battle."

Tucker maintains that a large percentage of the Texan garrison, perhaps even the majority, "fled in multiple attempts to escape the slaughter, trying to quit the compound before the battle inside had ended." He claims that fort's defense was "surprisingly weak, even feeble."

The evidence that Crockett initially survived is in an 1836 memoir by José Enrique de la Peña (a Mexican soldier who was at the siege and its aftermath) that was not published in English until 1975. According to that account, Crockett was one of a small handful of Texans who were either captured or surrendered after the battle, but were then executed by the infamous General Antonio López de Santa Anna.

According to Michael Lind in *The Wilson Quarterly,* the veracity of the "last stand" depends on whether the book (which didn't appear until 1955, via a Mexico City antiques dealer) really is "the work of de la Peña, *and* if de la Peña was telling the truth, *and* if he knew who Davy Crockett was. Skeptics have questioned all three of these assumptions." Unfortunately, most of the other contemporary accounts are no more definitive.

Interestingly, the idea of Crockett being captured after the battle is backed up in a Hamlin Garland introduction to a 1923 edition of the great man's own biography. The prose is somewhat purple. "At dawn on the sixth of March, 1836," the introduction says, "Crockett with five undaunted companions was captured by General Castrillon of the Mexican army. With a bloody bandage around his brow (he had been slashed by a saber) Crockett and his companions stood behind a barricade of those who had fallen before their weapons," it says, citing the 1848 pseudo-autobiographical *Col. Crockett's Exploits*.

Before going down, Crockett, according to this account, "sprang like a tiger at the ruffian [General Santa Anna, who ordered his execution] but before he could reach him a dozen swords were sheathed in his indomitable heart; and he fell, and died without a groan, a frown on his brow, and a smile of scorn and defiance on his lips."

There are multiple accounts that say Crockett survived the battle at the Alamo. These include, in addition to de la Peña, George M. Dolson, a so-called "Texian" Army sergeant who made his testimony in 1836; and Ramon Martinez Caro, who was General Santa Anna's secretary during the campaign in Texas.

Dolson says (interpreting the testimony of an unnamed Mexican officer who was there), that six prisoners, including Crockett, were brought before Santa Anna, who exclaimed, "Who has given you orders to take prisoners? I do not want to see those men living—shoot them."

Caro says there were only five prisoners captured, but the results were the same— with Santa Anna reprimanding the men for not killing the Texans on the spot. And then, "The soldiers stepped out of their ranks and set upon the prisoners until they were all killed."

There are discrepancies in the accounts, though they're alike in the main points. But there are also other Mexican eyewitness accounts that say Crockett died fighting. Sergeant Felix Nuñez was interviewed in 1889 (when he was eighty-four), and he says he saw "a tall American of rather dark complexion [who] had on a long *cuera* (buckskin coat) and a round cap without any bill, and made of fox skin, with the long tail hanging down his back."

Nuñez said, "This man apparently had a charmed life." Every soldier was aiming for him, but all missed. "On the contrary, [Crockett] never missed a shot. He killed at least eight of our men, besides wounding several others." Crockett was finally taken down by a lieutenant with a sword in this account, "and in an instant he was pierced by not less than twenty bayonets."

Susanna Dickinson, widow of the Alamo's artillery commander, Almeron Dickinson, said she saw Crockett lying dead between the church and the barrack building, his "peculiar cap" by his side.

To all this add the fact that de la Peña's account was famously challenged by Bill Groneman, author of several books on the Alamo. Examining the de la Peña manuscript at the University of Texas in 1991 and 1992 and later writing a book about it, he found such discrepancies as varied handwriting, ink, and paper types; errors of facts and anachronistic use of phrases; and, despite an 1836 date, references to sources that the author could not have then known existed.

Groneman concluded that the diary was faked in the twentieth century, with the forger John Laflin as a likely culprit. In 1998, however, the paper was authenticated as of a type used by the Mexican army and appropriate for the period. The diary was later sold at auction for $350,000.

Dr. James E. Crisp, a North Carolina State professor and author of *Sleuthing the Alamo: Davy Crockett's Last Stand and Other Mysteries of the Texas Revolution*, rebutted Groneman in a 1994 *Southwestern Historical Quarterly* article. He said Groneman "has employed considerable imagination (not to say credulity) in stretching thin and resistant

*Crockett at the Alamo. There's several versions about how it
ended. (Alamy Stock)*

THE COONSKIN CAP

The actual coonskin cap worn by Fess Parker in *Disneyland*'s *Davy Crockett* TV show is on display at the North Carolina Museum of History. It was donated by Parker in 2004, and was fashioned out of a real raccoon, retaining the poor animal's face.

The show, of course, wasn't exactly faithful to history. There are no period images of Davy Crockett wearing a coonskin cap. The strongest case he ever did is made by his daughter Matilda, who said that when her father left Tennessee for Texas in 1835, "He was dressed in his hunting suit, wearing a coonskin cap, and carrying a fine rifle presented to him by friends in Philadelphia."

But Matilda's observation isn't considered all that reliable—it was made many years after the actual event, and by that time the popular press had already put the fur hat firmly on Crockett's head. Perhaps such a fur piece was his idea of what a well-dressed Texan wore on his head? Could he have worn it there and hardly anywhere else?

The *Davy Crockett* series was a huge hit when it was shown as a five-part serial on the *Disneyland* show then turned into a pair of movies. The result of all that exposure was a coonskin cap craze—at one point in the mid-1950s, these faux fur headpieces were selling at a rate of five thousand per day. There was even a white "Polly Crockett" girls' model.

The craze was over by the end of the decade, when the *Davy Crockett* show went off the air. But the Alamo gift shop still sells fifteen thousand of those caps annually—it's the bestseller there. Billy Bob Thornton, who played Crockett in the 2004 remake of *The Alamo*, says he had a coonskin cap when he was a kid. "We all wanted to be Davy Crockett," he said. "I had a Davy Crockett outfit." With the cap? "Absolutely. But mine didn't have the whole face on it."

We know that Daniel Boone never wore a coonskin cap (he liked felt hats), but when Fess Parker—yes, the same guy—portrayed him on *Daniel Boone* (a TV series that ran for a healthy 165 episodes, from 1964 to 1970), he sported one. If you're a baby boomer who grew up glued to the tube, you're forgiven for confusing these two frontiersman.

The coonskin cap was ubiquitous in 1950s America. (Alamy Stock)

evidence to fit his twin theses that the diary is a forgery and that David Crockett died in combat."

None of this proves anything, one way or the other, and—given the stakes involving an icon of the American frontier—a resolution isn't possible. Crockett either went down swinging Old Betsy, or he was executed later. But in either case he was a stalwart defender of the Alamo.

WHAT HE SAID

The Autobiography of David [not Davy] *Crockett*, which he more than likely didn't write, is hardly a fount of wilderness lore. In fact (as in many mountain man narratives), much attention is devoted to killing anything that moves, especially bears. In fact, Crockett somewhat fancifully claims to have killed 105 in the same year. Here's a typically florid passage:

> I saw in and about the biggest bear that ever was seen in America. He looked, at the distance he was from me, like a large black bull. . . . In a little time I saw the bear climbing up a large black oak-tree, and I crawled on till I got within about eighty yards of him. He was setting with his breast to me; and so I put fresh priming in my gun, and fired at him. At this he raised one of his paws and snorted loudly. I loaded again as quick as I could, and fired as near the same place in his breast as possible. At the crack of my gun he came tumbling down; and the moment he touched the ground, I heard one of my best dogs cry out. I took my tomahawk in one hand, and my big butcher-knife in the other, and run up within four or five paces of him, at which he let my dog go, and fixed his eyes on me. I got back in all sorts of a hurry, for I know'd if he got hold of me, he would hug me altogether too close for comfort. I went to my gun and hastily loaded her again, and shot him the third time, which killed him good.

Exactly why Crockett feels the need to kill so many bears isn't made clear—it doesn't appear to have been for food—but our wilderness history is certainly replete with countless examples of pointless, wholesale slaughter as part of winning the West. The story of the buffalo's near-extermination at the hands of white gunmen (many shooting as many as they could from passing trains) is our best-known example. In that way, Davy Crockett was certainly a man of his time.

DAVY CROCKETT ON FILM

In 1955, *The New York Times* reviewed *Davy Crockett, King of the Wild Frontier* (assembled from the popular TV show) and proclaimed it "a straight juvenile entertainment with a story-line as simple as a T and enough poker-faced exaggeration to satisfy the most implausible fibber in school. The incidents are tall and transparent. No psychological subtleties to confuse. You know what's happening every single second."

This Davy, played by Fess Parker, is an aw-shucks backwoods scout who—when he's not hunting Creek Indians—is trying to "grin a b'ar" to death. And why not? It works on 'coons.

There was an actual Red Stick War (also known as the Creek War) between 1813 and 1814, a civil war between pro- and anti-white factions. Andrew Jackson, with Crockett along as a scout, forced the Creeks to sign a treaty in 1814, but then made little distinction between the groups that had fought with him and against him. Some 1.9 million of the 23 million acres he took (half of Alabama and part of southern Georgia) were from factions that had fought alongside the soldiers.

"Thus, Jackson converted the Creek civil war into an enormous land grab that ensured the ultimate destruction of the whole Creek Nation," wrote Robert V. Remini in his biography, *The Course of an American Empire*. The Cherokees, also Jackson's allies, were similarly mistreated. Crockett and others were even accused of stealing hogs from friendly Cherokee farmers while on the march back to Fort Strother.

In the Disney film, Red Stick is the leader of the renegades, and Crockett bests him in a hand-to-hand tomahawk fight, then—after sparing his life—convinces his foe to give up the battle. "I promise that the government will let you go back and live in peace on your own land," Crockett says, and they shake on it.

Red Stick actually has it right the first time. "White government lie," he said. "Davy Crockett don't lie," he's told, and that's apparently enough. But the treaty Jackson signed with the Creeks was ultimately a disaster for all Native Americans in the South and Southwest, Remini wrote.

It's interesting that much later, Crockett was at odds with Jackson because of the latter's anti-Indian policies—particularly the removal of the Cherokees from Oklahoma. He thought that Martin Van Buren would continue Jackson's cruelties, and so Crockett wrote in an 1834 letter, "Before I will Submit to his Government I will go to the wildes of Texas." It was not an idle boast.

In 1950, George Montgomery starred in *Davy Crockett, Indian Scout*, and here he's the old frontiersman's nephew, and he's got a sidekick named Red Hawk (brought up by missionaries) who cheerfully goes into battle against other tribes.

And Davy shows up, of course, in the many films about the Alamo. Perhaps the most memorable Davy was John Wayne in 1960 film *The Alamo*, attired in a coonskin cap and going down swinging a flaming torch. In the 1955 *The Last Command*, Jim Bowie wreaks havoc from his sick bed, and a bearded Crockett swings Old Betsy. In both films, the Mexican death count is in the hundreds, if not thousands. It seems excessive, but the actual number of casualties was around 600 (killed or wounded), compared to 182 to 257 Texans.

The Alamo was remade in 2004, with a more authentic Crockett played by a cap- and buckskin-free Billy Bob Thornton, who said it was his favorite role, ever.

David Crockett was indeed a popular and prolific writer, but his pen was probably never near most of what is attributed to him, particularly later works. Accuracy wasn't at a high premium in the first half of the nineteenth century. And there was money to be made. "Books about *Davy* Crockett [emphasis in the original], the 'ring-tailed roarer' from Tennessee, sold well," according to the *Reader's Companion to American History.*

For example, the popular *Crockett Almanac* of 1840 contains what is purported to be his first-person account, in dialect, of a shooting match with the legendary riverman Mike Fink (who, as we'll see, got around).

First, Crockett neatly shoots the ears off an unfortunate cat sitting on a fence, but Fink counters by docking the tails off a litter of pigs. "He hadn't left one of them pigs enough tail to make a toothpick on," the admiring Crockett notes. And when Fink shoots his wife's comb off her head "without stirring a hair," he wins the contest.

There's no actual evidence that Davy Crockett ever met Mike Fink, but then there's no definitive evidence that Mike Fink ever even existed.

Let's give Crockett the last word. He supposedly said of himself, to the US Congress no less, "I can walk like an ox, run like a fox, swim like an eel, yell like an Indian, fight like a devil, spout like an earthquake, make love like a mad bull, and swallow an Injun [other sources say "a nigger"] whole without choking if you butter his head and pin his ears back."

LEWIS AND CLARK

DISCOVERING WHAT WAS

ALREADY THERE

CAPTAIN MERIWETHER LEWIS AND
SECOND LIEUTENANT WILLIAM CLARK

THE LEGEND

In 1802, Napoléon Bonaparte sold the new United States the Louisiana Territory, encompassing an amazing 828,000 square miles, for $15 million. It wasn't considered a bargain, since $15 million was twice the federal budget at the time. And there was great uncertainty about what exactly had just been purchased.

Just two years later, President Thomas Jefferson sent Lewis (an explorer, soldier, and personal secretary to Jefferson) and Clark (a frontiersman who'd both fought and negotiated with native tribes) on a voyage of discovery that encompassed eight thousand miles of uncharted wilderness, traveling down the Ohio River then up the Missouri, across the Continental Divide all the way to the Pacific Ocean. As scientists, traders, and mapmakers, they helped define and bring (for better or worse) "civilization" to the vast territory west of the Mississippi River.

The goal was physically impossible—a water route to the Pacific coast that would greatly increase trade in these days before automobiles and paved roads. Jefferson thought that $2,500 and a party of twelve men would take care of it. He told Lewis and Clark, to "explore the Missouri River, & such principal stream of it, as, by its course and communication with the waters of the Pacific ocean . . . may offer the most direct and practicable water communication across this continent for the purpose of commerce."

They were gone for more than two years, and when they returned—with more than five thousand pages of journal entries, legal claims, a revelatory map of the American continent showing its topography and principal rivers, countless scientific specimens, and new relationships with two dozen Indian nations (whose artifacts they also collected)—they were properly lionized as outstanding pioneers who brought light to dark regions.

Meriwether Lewis. He was an explorer, soldier, and personal secretary to Jefferson. (Library of Congress)

HOW THEY GET IT WRONG

Much of the territory Lewis and Clark explored had, of course, already been extensively traveled and settled by Native tribes, and neither were they the first white people on the scene—fur trappers and traders had often gotten there before them.

The French established posts on the Mississippi's shores in the seventeenth and eighteenth centuries, after the 1682 voyage of René-Robert Cavelier, Sieur de La Salle from the Great Lakes to the Gulf of Mexico. La Salle named "La Louisiane" (for Louis XIV), established relations with many Native tribes, and eventually controlled a vast fur trade. His untimely demise came in 1687, after his crew mutinied on an ill-fated mission to establish a French presence in the Gulf—and wrest control of Mexico from Spain.

The mouth of the Columbia River had been discovered, mapped, and claimed for the US by Robert Gray in 1792. In 1789 and 1793, on behalf of the North West Company in two epic journeys, the Scottish-born Alexander Mackenzie reached the Pacific and the Arctic Ocean from Quebec.

The 1789 expedition to the Arctic Ocean traversed three thousand miles of Canadian wilderness, but Mackenzie didn't get there on his own. He brought with him Nestabeck, a Chippewa guide who was known as the "English Chief." On the second expedition, which reached the Pacific in July of 1793, Mackenzie was advised on the best route by British Columbia's Carrier (or Dakelh) Indians, and borrowed canoes from the Nuxalk (or Bella Coola).

Lewis and Clark had native guides, too. Only recently, with a more enlightened attitude toward Native Americans, has the true role of the Shoshone Sacagawea (brought into the expedition by her husband, trapper Toussaint Charbonneau) been recognized. Sacagawea wasn't a guide, but she helped the Corps forage for local food and plant-based medicines, was an important interpreter and negotiator for the Corps' dealings with Native tribes, and assisted them in obtaining horses from her family band of Shoshone when they were vitally needed.

According to *Lewis and Clark Through Indian Eyes*, when the explorers arrived in Shoshone territory, they encountered a people who had already been decimated by a smallpox epidemic that killed as many as fifty thousand Native Americans from the northern and southern plains after emerging in 1780. Half the Shoshone reportedly died.

Smallpox had visited the tribes of the upper Missouri River before Lewis and Clark, but it was even worse afterwards. According to the State Historical Society of North Dakota,

"Lewis and Clark at Three Forks," with Sacagawea. This is a detail of a 1912 mural by Edgar Samuel Paxson in the Montana State House of Representatives. (Wikipedia photo)

> For Native Peoples, the aftermath of the Lewis and Clark [expedition] was anything but a positive experience. Perhaps the most devastating was the outbreak of smallpox among the Mandan in 1837, an epidemic which all but destroyed the once-powerful group.... [C]onsiderable numbers of Hidatsa were similarly affected.

Lewis records in his journal of August 14, 1805, that the Shoshone were already quite familiar with the Spanish (whose territory then encompassed much of what is now the western US), and complained that these other white people wouldn't give them firearms and ammunition for fear they would "kill each other." Lewis saw

Spanish brands on the horses, mules obtained from the same source, and "a bridle bit of [S]panish manufactory."

In October that year, the expedition's John Ordway described encountering tribes with "pleanty of beeds Copper & brass trinkets" which they'd obtained "from Some tradors on a River to the North of this place." He further describes seeing "a number of articles which came from white people," including copper kettles.

Despite this evidence, historical accounts often imply that Lewis and Clark met uncontacted tribes. For instance, PBS reports the encounter this way: "Lewis and his men were the first white people the Shoshones had ever seen." That may have been true of these Shoshone, but white people had already made a big impression on the plains tribes. Lewis also complained, despite their ownership of four hundred "fine" horses, of the "extreem poverty of these poor people."

Mark N. Trahant, a Shoshone-Bannock Indian and the Charles R. Johnson Professor of Journalism at the University of North Dakota, argues that Lewis and Clark's portrait was misleading, ignoring the negative effects of the smallpox epidemic and downplaying the political organization of the tribe. "The Shoshone band that met the Corps of Discovery already had a democratic system in place," he said.

Writing about the Walla Walla, Cayuse, and Umatilla ancestors that Ordway described, Roberta Conner of the Confederated Tribes of the Umatilla Indian Reservation points out, "When Lewis and Clark and the Corps of Discovery arrived in our homeland in October of 1805, our people had lived in this place for thousands of years, had intertribal trade alliances, reciprocity agreements for safe passage, and we had conducted multi-tribal expeditions to distant lands. We had white man's goods in the mid-Columbia Plateau."

WHAT WE ACTUALLY KNOW

Lewis and Clark's achievements were considerable, but shouldn't be exaggerated. In an introduction to *Lewis & Clark: The Journey of the Corps of Discovery* by Ken Burns and Dayton Duncan, the historian Bernard DeVoto writes that they were "the first United States citizens to experience the Great Plains," and the first to see "the daunting peaks of the Rocky Mountains." That's true, but that "US citizens" is quite a qualifier. Other Americans not given the privilege of citizenship had seen those sights many times.

The settled US was quite small in 1801, when Thomas Jefferson became president. Two of every three Americans lived within fifty miles of the Atlantic, and the Mississippi was the western border. Jefferson

William Clark was the frontiersman on the expedition. (Library of Congress photo)

himself had never been more than fifty miles west of the Shenandoah Valley, so it's not surprising he would want to see the West mapped and explored. The hope was for an easy and navigable route to Asian trade routes.

On May 14, 1804, the expedition set out on the Missouri River paddling two flat-bottomed canoes and a fifty-five-foot keelboat that Mike Fink would have recognized. They went under "a jentle brease," accompanied by a Newfoundlander named Seaman.

Sergeant Patrick Gass summed up the great unknown that was ahead. "The best authenticated accounts informed us," he said,

> that we were to pass through a country possessed by numerous, powerful
> and warlike nations of savages, of gigantic stature, fierce, treacherous
> and cruel; and particularly hostile to white men. . . . The determined
> and resolute character, however, of the corps, and the confidence which
> pervaded all ranks dispelled every emotion of fear, and anxiety for the
> present; while a sense of duty, and of the honour, which would attend
> the completion of the object of the expedition; a wish to gratify the
> expectations of the government, and of our fellow citizens, with the feelings
> which novelty and discovery invariably inspire, seemed to insure to us
> ample support in our future toils, suffering and dangers.

It rained a lot. The men suffered from all kinds of minor injuries, such as dislocated shoulders, sunstroke, and snakebites, which were treated by Lewis (who'd had medical training). They were also much plagued by mosquitoes. Several men received court martial sentences for getting drunk, and received fifty to one hundred lashes. Near the present-day Sioux City, Iowa, in August, Sergeant Charles Floyd, a quartermaster, died of what Lewis said was "bilious cholic."

Floyd, who died with what Clark said was "a great deal of composure," was the expedition's only fatality, and the first American soldier to die west of the Mississippi.

The principal message may have been furthering trade, but natural history got its due—the Corps brought back 178 plants and 122 animals previously undescribed, including such iconic western species as the mountain goat, the antelope, and the bighorn sheep. A prairie dog and a magpie made it back alive; the rest were stuffed. A Clark entry for May 31, 1804, reads in part, "Several rats of Considerable Size was Cought in the woods to day—Capt Lewis went out to the woods & found many

A statue of Meriwether Lewis (in hat) and William Clark outside the Lewis & Clark Interpretive Center in Sioux City, Iowa. (Library of Congress photo)

"Spirit of Discovery"
by Pat Kennedy
2002

Commissioned by
Missouri River Historical Development, Inc.

Art Consultant: Steven Boody

curious Plants & Srubs, one Deer killed this evening." Deer meat was important to sustain the group, though they would later have more exotic fare—buffalo, especially.

In August, the Corps encountered both Sioux and Omaha Indians, and gave them presents designed to impress them with the wealth and technical power of the white man's nation. Firearms demonstrations were effective. Lewis and Clark were following Jefferson's instruction to learn as much as they could about the tribes encountered, and prepare them for a trading relationship.

The encounters were friendly, and the tribes often made gifts of food (including dogs) to the travelers. They were welcomed in the Mandan villages on the Upper Missouri, and built Fort Mandan on their territory (at present-day Washburn, North Dakota, thirty-eight miles north of Bismarck) as a haven against winter temperatures that reached forty degrees below zero Fahrenheit.

The Mandans gave whites the name Mací, meaning "nice people," and helped the

explorers draw up maps of the lands to the west. Burns and Duncan write, "Though a handful of tribes had never seen white people before they met Lewis and Clark, all of them had already been affected by the three-hundred-year presence of Europeans on the continent." As a case in point, the Corps visited the grave of one Blackbird, an Omaha chief who was killed in a smallpox epidemic.

In the end, only two Indians died as a result of encounters with the Corps, which is remarkable considering the bloody conflicts that were to come. Sacagawea ("Bird Woman") had been with the company as the wife of fur trader Charbonneau since November of 1804, and on February 11, 1805, she delivered a child. Lewis said the long labor was "tedious," but eased by the administration of "a small portion of the rattle from a rattlesnake."

The importance of sixteen-year-old Sacagawea to the expedition was not yet clear, since Lewis then refers to her only as "one of the wives of Charbono." Indeed, the Frenchman had likely bought her (and another Indian wife) from the Minnetarees, who'd held her in captivity. But by August, the Corps had encountered their first Shoshone, Sacagawea's people. They needed horses to cross the Rockies, and Sacagawea was most helpful here—because the tribe's chief was Cameahwait, her brother. "The meeting of those two people was really affecting," Lewis wrote. "She made signs to me that they were her nation," Clark added.

Sacagawea was not the Corp's guide, but she was invaluable in foraging for local foods, including wild artichokes, roots, goose eggs, currants, and prairie turnips. She also found plants with medicinal properties, such as fennel root for stomach aches and camas root for strength. And her very presence—a Native woman among all the whites—was vital in easing negotiations with the tribes they met.

When the Corps reached the mouth of the Columbia River on the Pacific Coast on November 20, 1805, they attempted to buy a sea otter robe for President Jefferson, but the Indians would accept payment only in blue beads. So Sacagawea gave up her beaded belt. When her husband, an incompetent at the helm of a boat, foundered his pirogue,

A recreation of Lewis and Clark's quarters at Fort Mandan.
(Wikipedia photo)

it was Sacagawea who managed to retrieve vital navigational instruments and books that were aboard.

On the return trip, in July of 1806, Sacagawea again proved invaluable in locating a pass through the Rocky Mountains. Clark: "The Indian woman informed me that she had been in this plain frequently and knew it well. . . . She said we would discover a gap in the mountains in our direction . . ." Only seven days later, she supplied a route for crossing into the Yellowstone River basin, later to be the path of the Northern Pacific Railway across the Continental Divide.

Near the end of the trip, Clark wrote to Charbonneau. "Your woman who accompanied you that long dangerous and fatigueing rout to the Pacific Ocian and back diserved a greater reward for her attention and services on that rout than we had in our power to give her at the Mandans," he said. Clark offered to take Sacagewea's son (who he called "Pomp" or "Pompey," though his name was Jean-Baptiste) and "raise him as my own child."

Sacagawea did indeed come to St. Louis with Jean-Baptiste and Charbonneau in 1809. Clark took charge of the boy's education and enrolled him in a boarding school. Sacagawea had a daughter, Lizette, in 1810. She may have died at Fort Manuel (where the Bighorn and Yellowstone rivers come together) of what was described as "putrid fever" in 1812.

But there's an alternative version. Sacagawea reportedly had expressed the desire to return to her native country, and maybe she did. We know that Charbonneau lived a long life, since he was spotted asking for an Indian Bureau pension in 1839. The account of Sacagawea's death in 1812 is from a clerk at the fort, and he identifies the deceased only as "the wife of Charbonneau, a Snake squaw." But the French-Canadian trader had a lot of wives, and it could have been the one known as Otter Woman. Shoshonis were often identified as "Snake" at the time.

In the 1920s, Dr. Charles A. Eastman, of Sioux descent and an authority on the Western Plains tribes, investigated and put together a narrative that had Sacagawea

"Lewis and Clark on the Lower Columbia" (1905) by Charles Marion Russell. (Wikipedia photo)

leaving Charbonneau (because of his frequent beatings) and spending time among many different tribes, including the Kiowas, the Comanches and the Wichitas, before finally returning to her own tribe at the Wind River reservation at Fort Washakie. In this account, she died in 1884, a respected elder who proudly displayed her Jefferson medal.

So what happened to Clark's "Pompey"? Jean-Baptiste was taken in by Clark (as was Lizette), and the young hero of the expedition was sent to good schools in St. Louis. Then, in 1823, he met Duke Friedrich Paul Wilhelm of Württemberg, nephew of the king, who took Jean-Baptiste to Europe—where he lived the royal life for six years.

Back in the US as a linguist with a classical education, Sacagawea's son returned to his roots and became a trapper, scout (including in the Mexican-American War), prospector and even (briefly) mayor, who encountered Jim Bridger, John Frémont, and James Beckwourth. According to Dale L. Walker's *Legends and Lies*, Jean-Baptiste Charbonneau was a charming man of two worlds, "comfortable among Indians and whites alike." He may have died of pneumonia in Oregon in 1866, or survived until 1885 on the Wind River reservation, dying there a year after his mother.

Little is known about Lizette Charbonneau; she may have died in childhood.

All of this is not to suggest that history should record the expedition of "Lewis and Clark and Sacagawea," but that Native American contribution to the ultimate success of their journey should not be underestimated. Lewis and Clark returned as national heroes, feted at balls everywhere they went, and were rewarded with 1,600 acres of prime land each. The Indians who'd helped the Corps along the way didn't share in the spoils.

Also not seeing a reward was York, Clark's black slave—who'd been the subject of much amazement to the Indians who encountered him. Hidatsa chief Le Borgne, never having seen an African-American before, reportedly tried to see if the color would wipe off.

The Corps was met with wild acclaim when it returned to St. Louis. According to Richard Edwards' 1860 history of the city, *Edwards's Great West*, "Even the negro York, who was the body servant of Clark, despite his ebony complexion, was looked upon with decided partiality, and received his share of adulation." But when the cheering stopped York returned to ten more years of slavery before Clark freed him.

Some accounts say that York then chose to live among the Indians who treated him with respect, but this is probably wishful thinking. He actually went into the freight business, at which some say he fared poorly. Clark told Washington Irving that York was on his way back to service with his old master in St. Louis when he died, reportedly of cholera, in 1832. There's no definitive account of what happened to York, but it's safe to say that service in the Corps of Discovery was the high point of a life that was seriously constrained by the facts of life in pre-Civil War America.

WHAT THEY SAID

Two quotes associated with Sacagawea are "Everything I do is for my people" and "Don't go around saying the world owes you a living," though the latter one, at least, sounds suspiciously contemporary.

Clark is famous for prematurely proclaiming, on November 7, 1805, "Ocian in view! O! the joy." Actually, they were at the estuary of the Columbia River, and 20 miles from the coast. The actual Pacific was reached in the middle of the month.

On January 6, 1806, Sacagawea made her case for being part of a party that was going to dip their toes in the Pacific. Clark wrote in his journal, "She observed that She had traveled a long way with us to See the great waters, and that now that monstrous fish was also to be Seen, She thought it verry hard that She Could not be permitted to See either (She had never yet been to the Ocian)."

THE LEWIS AND CLARK TRAIL

Up for a 3,700-mile adventure? You can recreate the famous expedition by following the National Park Service's Lewis and Clark National Historic Trail. It duplicates the route the pair took between 1804 and 1806—starting in Wood River, Illinois, and proceeding all the way to the Columbia River's mouth in Oregon.

There are twenty-three National Historic Trails, and Lewis and Clark's is the second longest. If you're really ambitious, you can start in Washington, DC, because that's where Lewis traveled from in March of 1803, preparing himself for his western adventure. But the more likely departure date is May 14, 1804, when the Corps left St. Louis on its way up the Missouri River. So you can start from there if you'd like.

Most modern travelers drive (taking the family RV is popular), but you'd get extra points for walking, portaging, and floating, as the original explorers did. There are, of course, historical markers all along the trail, and restored forts and visitors' centers at many sites.

The Facebook page for the trail is fascinating, containing entries like this one, "If Captain Lewis were to pick up a pizza this weekend, he'd probably order it with anchovies. One of the fish that Captain Lewis enjoyed, especially when cooked by the Clatsop Indians, was the eulachon, or candlefish, a member of the smelt family." Lewis wrote in February of 1806 that he liked them best "cooked in Indian stile."

Sacagawea is showcased on U-Haul trucks, but she's not
nearly as famous as Pocahontas.
(U-Haul image, used by permission)

This Sacagawea statue is in the Shoshone Tribal Cemetery
in Fort Washakie, Wyoming. (Library of Congress)

POCAHONTAS AND SACAGAWEA AS MERCHANDISE

When it comes to the most famous Native
American women, Pocahontas—the subject of
an idealized Disney movie—definitely has the
edge. And it shows in the shameless commerce
department.

There's not a lot of Sacagawea merchandise.
Although her image is on an (unpopular)
dollar coin, and she's featured as #117 in the
U-Haul Venture Across America truck mural
series for Montana, only a few commemorative
T-shirts (and a $32 chiffon top) are available.

But when it comes to Pocahontas, the
sky's the limit: keychains, dolls, posters,
bows, fringed dresses, necklaces, "Colors of
the Wind" pendants, decals, DVDs, Indian
Princess mouse ears, clocks, paper napkins . . .
. A Disney T-shirt has an image of the Native
American superstar looking like a runway
model, with the legend, "Sometimes the Right
Path Is Not the Easiest."

In the Disney version at least, Pocahontas is
a nature goddess and a princess, who sacrifices
for her Romeo and Juliet–style love, John
Smith. But even in legend, Sacagawea didn't
have something going with Lewis or Clark.
She wasn't actually a guide, though many
images show her with an arm outstretched,
pointing the way forward. And at the end of
the Corps' epic journey, she just disappears.

Hollywood doesn't seem much interested
in Sacagawea as a movie star, though a 2004
PBS documentary narrated by Rita Coolidge
is available. It "seeks the woman behind the
historical icon."

MIKE FINK

MORE TALL TALE
THAN MAN

MIKE FINK

THE LEGEND

Mike Fink was the king of the Mississippi keelboaters in the days before steam. He was half alligator and half horse, and he could "outrun, outhop, out-jump, throw down, drag out, and lick any man in the country!" He was a dead shot (puncturing cups of whiskey on his friends' heads), and he and his pal Davy Crockett used to hold shooting contests. In one story, Fink shot the corkscrew tails off four pigs. Crockett thereupon declared he'd left too much of a stub, and shot those off also. The Mike Fink seen in Disney's *Davy Crockett and the River Pilots* is all bluster, though a pretty good shot and a very capable river pilot.

Mike Fink may never have existed, but he's definitely a larger-than-life legend. (Alamy Stock)

HOW THEY GET IT WRONG

The first thing you have to accept about Mike Fink is that he may never have existed, at least not in the form in which he's come down to us. The historical record is scant, even his name, which is sometimes spelled "Micke Phinck." Once you accept the concept of a wild man who did everything to incredible excess—and better than anyone else—the teller of tall tales can take it from there. Eudora Welty wrote about him, as did Carl Sandburg, and he also appears in Orson Scott Card's *The Tales of Alvin Maker*.

According to the 1956 *Half Horse Half Alligator: The Growth of the Mike Fink Legend*, tall tales tend to cluster around certain figures, and their number includes half the characters that are the subject of this book—and especially Davy Crockett, Daniel Boone, and Mike Fink.

"Printed stories as well as oral traditions contributed to Fink's fame," *Half Horse Half Alligator* notes. "In some instances, authors, one is sure, based their statements about oral traditions upon published claims rather than upon personal experiences. In other instances, authors may well have invented stories on their own or may have adapted to Fink printed or oral tales originally told about others."

Crockett was "a suitable peg upon which almanac makers hang a host of anecdotes originally attributed to others," authors Walter Blair and Franklin J. Meine write, and so was Mike Fink. His life, what we know of it, is perfect for embroidery, embracing as it does the Revolutionary War, the glory days of the Mississippi River, and a career-ending stint as a scout among the trappers and mountain men of the Rockies.

Fink stories go back a long, long way. Carl Sandburg, in his bestselling Abraham Lincoln biography, writes about the sixteen-year-old future president working on a ferryboat that crossed the Ohio River in 1825. "Occasionally came a customer who looked as if he might be one of the 'half-horse, half-alligator men' haunting the Ohio water course in those years. There was river talk about Mike Fink . . . the toughest of the crowd . . . a famous marksman and fighter."

Fink was alleged to have been a great friend of Davy Crockett. (Wikipedia)

An actual sighting might have been nice, but that's the way it is with Mike Fink. Instead of facts, we have stories—hundreds of them circulating while Fink was supposedly still alive. Getting a fix on him is like tailing the historical William Shakespeare, or Jesus of Nazareth. So here are some stories.

Morgan Neville's 1828 "The Last of the Boatmen" describes a close encounter near a boat landing with an approximately fifty-year-old Fink, who was wearing red flannel, "moccasins and a broad leathern belt, from which hung suspended in a sheath a large knife." Fink promptly shoots a cup off his brother's head before an admiring crowd. "A thousand legends illustrate the fearlessness of his character," Neville wrote.

An 1829 account in *The Western Monthly Review* describes Fink, warned not to shoot a mother sow and her eight or nine piglets on the riverbank, instead taking pleasure in merely shooting off their curly tails. "Mike . . . laid his rifle to his face and shot at each pig successively, as the boat glided up the river under easy sail, about 40 or 50 yards from shore, and cut off their tails close to their rumps, without doing them any other harm."

What's funny about this story of porcine indignities is that, as noted, it appeared again a decade later in the *Crockett Almanac*, not on the river but as the *coup de grâce* that allowed Fink to beat the redoubtable Davy in a shooting contest. Of course, he might have performed the same trick more than once—there were a lot of pigs around in those days, and plenty of bullets.

Here's a colorful description of Fink, probably transposed and paraphrased from the first person and reprinted in a 1934 edition of the *Record Journal* of Douglas, Colorado.

He was half wild horse and half cock-eyed alligator, and the rest of him was crooked snags and red-hot snappin' turtle. He was a Salt River roarer. He was a ring-tailed squealer, a reg'lar screamer from the ol' Mississip'. He was nursed on a bottle of rye before his eyes were opened. He loved the women and he was chock-full of fight. . . . He could out-run, out-jump, out-shoot, out-brag, out-drink and out-fight, rough and tumble, any man on both sides of the river from Pittsburgh to New Orleans and back ag'in to St. Louis.

Almanac accounts describe Mike Fink fighting (and winning) a life-and-death bare-hands struggle with a wolf that jumped onto his boat, and dispatching a moose with his knife after no end of shenanigans.

One of the few vaguely historical records relating to Mike Fink is from St. Louis's *Western Souvenir* in 1829. The story describes him shooting off the rear end of a black man's bare foot in 1821 because he was offended by its African-derived shape. His defense was that he wanted to help the man "wear a decent boot." According to that account, Fink was tried in the circuit court, found guilty, and given an unknown punishment—but was free again by 1822.

Of course, that's hardly proof that the incident actually occurred—the *Western Souvenir* writer simply states, "I have myself seen the record of the court." The 1847 "Trimming a Darky's Heel" from the *Reveille* maintains that Fink evaded custody by paying off the officer who came to arrest him, and sending "a handful of silver to the darky to extract the pain from his shortened heel."

The same story occurs in many other sources with embellishments, such as the "facts" that the foot in question was more than one hundred yards away, and that the shot (delivered via his rifle, Betsy, the same name given to Crockett's firearm) removed part of the heel without damaging the bone. But the *Western Souvenir* says the victim was "badly wounded." And, not surprisingly, other sources give the name of Fink's rifle as "Old Bang-All."

WHAT WE ACTUALLY KNOW

We don't actually "know" anything about Mike Fink, because beyond the legends there isn't much definitive information at all. Fink was probably born (if he was actually born!) near Pittsburgh around 1770. He was a woodsman honing his marksmanship by shooting squirrels in his earliest incarnation, but by the time he was fifteen he was keelboating on the Ohio and Mississippi Rivers. By the early 1800s, he reportedly owned and captained a pair of boats out of Wheeling, West Virginia.

"The sound of the boat horn was his most entrancing music," claims Hiram Martin Chittenden in his 1902 "The Treachery of Mike Fink." He could supposedly imitate the horn's sound with his voice alone. Chittenden describes Fink as "a perfect model for Hercules," weighing about 180 pounds, five feet nine inches tall, with a broad, round face (tanned to a ruddy brown by the sun) and pleasant features that included bright blue eyes and "broad white teeth."

Fink made good money transporting goods down the Mississippi. This imposing figure was a regular in the taverns that did excellent business in all the riverfront towns, reportedly earning a pile of red feathers awarded to the men who showed the most prowess. Around this time he supposedly met Davy Crockett, who, according to the *Crockett Almanac* of 1840, wandered in to Fink's homestead looking for a place to spend the night. When they weren't shooting, the pair sat on Fink's porch, passing around a jug.

Crockett describes his friend, in that first-person almanac account, as a "helliferocious fellow," who was

> an almighty fine shot . . . Mike was an boatman on the Mississip, but he had
> a little cabbin on the head of the Cumberland, and a horrid handsome wife,
> that loved him the wickedest that ever you see. Mike only worked enough
> to find his wife in rags, and himself in powder, and lead, and whiskey, and
> the rest of the time he spent in nocking over bar and turkeys, and bouncing
> deer, and sometimes drawing a bead on an injun.

Fink's prowess with a gun was unmatched. At least that's what the tall tales say. (Alamy Stock)

MIKE FINK'S TALL TALES

The period *Crockett Almanac* compiled some interesting tales told on Mike Fink.

In 1850, it says, Fink set out to scare Davy Crockett's wife, and crept into an old alligator's skin. He surprised the unfortunate woman while on her evening constitutional. Being made of sterner stuff, Ms. Crockett knocked the alligator's head off "with a little teeth pick" and sent it flying fifty feet, shaving Fink's head in the process. Seeing who she was dealing with, the pioneer wife "rolled up her sleeves an battered poor Fink so that he fainted away in his alligator skin."

In 1851, the "celebrated" Fink "once observed some Indians stealing into a widow's milk-cave, from which they had frequently stolen quantities of cream, meat, cheese, &c. He watched them until they got in, fastened the door outside, and then bored holes through the bank above. He and his son then commenced pouring hot water down on them, until they yelled, kicked, and fainted; while those who could broke out, and ran off to the woods, half scalded, telling their people that the milk-cave rained hot water."

In 1852, Fink was attacked by a wolf "while in his very boat." Things looked dicey, but "our indomitable hero was not to be daunted by anything that threatened him—and he wrestled and tugged with his sturdy antagonist, till the beast foamed at the mouth, and howled—as if more under the effects of pain than rage." Fink managed to fling the wolf into the water, only to have it come after him again "with renewed fury." At last, the wolf was overboard and held under until he was "completely" drowned.

That same year, Fink was again in hand-to-hand combat with a wolf, but subdued it "with one terrible blow."

The reputed grave of Mike Fink, after he was reportedly killed in an altercation with local Indians in 1780. (Wikipedia)

Mike Fink's Great Shot.

Fink could shoot the tail off a pig, or give some poor unsuspecting soul a haircut. (Wikipedia)

Chittenden maintained that Fink first visited St. Louis in 1814 or 1815, and frequently thereafter. He also said it was common for Fink "to fill a tin cup with whiskey and shoot it from [his friends'] heads at a distance of 70 yards." In 1818, he was believed to be living in Missouri, and may be the same "Michael Fink" taken to court by one Nicholas Hartzel for refusing to pay a sixteen-dollar debt.

In 1822, with friend William Carpenter (one of the heads that held the whiskey cup), Fink reportedly joined a group of one hundred pioneers who answered an ad for one hundred "enterprizing [sic] young men" to "ascend the Missouri River to its source," and establish a fur trade in Montana. Joining Fink was the legendary mountain man Jedediah Smith, an abstemious frontiersman and trapper who was also a mapmaker and an early Rocky Mountains explorer.

That Fink was part of this expedition could well be apocryphal, since Fink was no spring chicken—he would have been over fifty by that time. But they did need an experienced riverman to take them up the Missouri River.

The book *Western Rivermen, 1763–1861* says that Fink "was supposedly an Indian fighter and scout, but there is no documented account of his activities. Evidently he was a remarkable shot and a fine hunter."

Fink was reportedly killed in 1823 in a feud with two trappers near Fort Henry, though *Western Rivermen* says there are "two dozen versions" of what actually happened—and maybe nothing did. The party, with Fink in tow, camped for the winter at the mouth of the Yellowstone River. Fink and Carpenter quarreled there, possibly over an Indian woman, but then made up their differences and decided to cement the friendship by shooting whiskey cups off each other's heads.

Fink took the first shot, after telling Carpenter not to spill the liquor because "I shall want some presently." Unfortunately, the legendary sharpshooter's aim failed him, and Carpenter took a bullet in the forehead. Carpenter's great friend Levi Talbot took offense at this turn of events and, some months later, shot Fink through the heart. "Mike fell and died without a word," Chittenden says.

A bare-bones account of these events for the Rocky Mountain Fur Company is reported in contemporary papers of General William Clark held by the Kansas Historical Society. "Mike Fink shot Carpenter—Talbot soon after shot Fink, and not long after was himself drowned at the Tetons," it says. But the account is dated 1822, when Fink and party were actually en route.

A rather gruesome endnote that may (or may not) confirm this account of the legend's death: Later in 1823, according to a report from the fort quoted in *Half Horse Half Alligator*, a party of Blackfeet Indians dug up the bodies of Fink and Carpenter. "According to their usual barbarity, they commenced to open the graves in order to strip the bodies of whatever clothes might be wrapped around them," the report said. "But finding they were in a putrid state, they left them without further molestation." Some thirty-five years later, interpreter Zephyr Rencontre pointed out Fink's grave site to A. H. Redfield, Indian agent for the Upper Missouri.

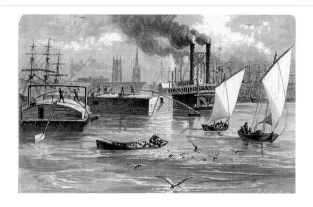

The Mississippi River at New Orleans, circa 1873. The busy port was a destination for cargo-carrying flatboats like those supposedly piloted by Mike Fink. (Woodcut by A. Measom, Jr./Wikipedia)

FLAT BOATS: THE WORLD MIKE FINK KNEW

Courtesy of the *Steamboat Times*, we have a very colorful history of flat boats on the Ohio and Mississippi Rivers. The first person to successfully navigate a flatboat from Brownsville, Pennsylvania, to New Orleans was Jacob Yoder in 1782. He was carrying flour.

Typically, flat or keelboats ("broadhorns," "Natchez boats" and "Kentucky boats" were other names) measured fifty-five feet long and sixteen feet wide. The cabin for people was in front, and the pen for animals in the back. A crew of four, plus a pilot like Fink, was most common. After steamboats became available (around 1840), they were often called "barges" and towed upriver. Before steam, the boats were usually dismantled in New Orleans.

Among the cargoes carried by flatboats were whiskey, hides, barrel staves (Davy Crockett's plan), lumber, honey, salt, apples, tobacco, poultry, and livestock. Carrying white horses or cows was believed to bring bad luck. A downriver trip took eight to twelve weeks, so whatever they carried had to survive without refrigeration.

Were there famous flatboat men besides Mike Fink? Certainly—Abraham Lincoln twice piloted flatboats from Illinois to New Orleans, in 1828 (barrel pork) and 1831 (corn, sides of bacon, barrel pork, and live hogs). On both trips, he saw the reality of southern slavery. The sight of it, he said, "was a continual torment to me."

It wasn't all work for the crew of keelboats. George Caleb Bingham's 1846 painting *The Jolly Rivermen*, made into a popular print, shows men dancing to a fiddle on a boat that's carrying furs and blankets. The National Gallery, which purchased the painting in 2015, considers it the most important genre painting in US history.

WHAT HE SAID

"I am a Salt River roarer, and I love the wimming, and as how I am chock full of fight."

This quote from Fink is from the 1842 *Spirit of the Times* story "The Disgraced Scalp-Lock" by Thomas Bangs Thorpe. "I'm a regular tornado, tough as a hickory withe, long winded as a nor'wester. I can strike a blow like a falling tree, and every lick makes a gap in the crowd that lets in an acre of sunshine. Whew, boys!" The scalp lock of the title belongs to an Indian, and Fink shoots it off without otherwise harming its owner.

"The Jolly Flatboatmen" by George Caleb Bingham, 1846. (Wikipedia)

JOHN "LIVER-EATING" JOHNSTON

OUT FOR

VENGEANCE

JOHN "LIVER-EATING" JOHNSTON
(AKA JOHN JOHNSON AND JEREMIAH JOHNSON)

"Liver-Eating" Johnston is one of frontier history's most misrepresented figures. (Photo 75.6059, Archives and Special Collections, Mansfield Library, University of Montana)

THE LEGEND

Jeremiah Johnson was a former sailor and a veteran of the Mexican War who became an accomplished mountain man and trapper, living by a strong moral code that turned the native tribes who came his way from murderous intent to grudging respect. He was forced to fight for his life, and lost his family, when the US Army troops he was guiding ignored his advice and disrespected a sacred Crow burial ground. Johnson avenged his family's deaths against overwhelming odds, and became a legend among the Indian tribes as a brave warrior.

In another version, John "Liver-Eating" Johnston (sometimes known as "Liver *Eater* Johnston") was a brave mountain man, whiskey trader, wood cutter, and trapper whose Indian wife and child were murdered by the Crows, hence his vow to kill as many Crows as possible and eat their livers. The exact number is unknown, but it was in the hundreds.

Neither of these legends—the first from a movie, the second from a novel—have much to do with the actual historical figure.

HOW THEY GET IT WRONG

When the popular image of Johnston is formed by Robert Redford in the title role of the 1972 film *Jeremiah Johnson*, it's likely that we're going to be carried far from the gritty frontier. The real "Jeremiah Johnson," whose name at birth may have been John Garrison (later changed to John Johnston), is said to have stood six feet two inches and weighed as much as 280 pounds, far more than Redford. Of course, he's also been described as shorter and weighing less.

The popular movie (directed by Sydney Pollack, though Francis Ford Coppola was associated with the project early on) credits and roughly follows the life story as outlined by Raymond Thorp and Robert Bunker in their dramatic 1958 book *Crow Killer: The Saga of Liver-Eating Johnson*. But, so as not to offend the sensibilities of the times, it keeps the revenge plot but leaves out both scalping and the critical liver eating (reportedly against the protests of screenwriter John Milius). It must be noted that— although there are pages on authoritative-sounding sources—the authors wrote a novel, complete with some pretty bad dialogue and abundant frontier racism.

Crow Killer's Johnston totes a Sharps buffalo gun and says things like "Cuss me fer a Kiowa!" and "Slicin' a man don't bother me none." The movie version is a man of few words, and of much more refined sensibilities. His fifty-caliber Hawken black powder rifle (which the real John Johnston also owned) was pried from the frozen corpse of one Hatchet Jack.

Jeremiah Johnson, which is probably better without the liver eating, also takes material from *Mountain Man*, a first-rate novel by Vardis Fisher first published in 1965. And it's from there that we get the film's vivid subplot (and dialogue) about Johnson coming upon, and later avenging, a bloodstained madwoman whose three children have just been slain by Indians near the Musselshell, a tributary of the Missouri River. Johnson is Samson Minard in that book. Fisher writes in the introduction that Sam is "drawn in some degree" from Johnston, and madwoman Kate Bowden from the real-life Jane

Morgan. "Though these two persons actually lived they are today almost completely lost in legends," the book says.

Since there's not a whole lot on the public record about John Johnston, one way or the other, *Crow Killer*, novel or not, stood as the real story for decades. And it established Johnston as a man of principle. "John Johnson is a man of sentiment and honor," the book says. "And for all his seeming savagery remains faithful to the code of the mountain man."

Sure, the book says Johnston killed "hundreds" of Crow Indians and ate their livers, but it was revenge for their murder of his Flathead wife and unborn child. And, of course, "For all the hundreds of scalps he acquired, Johnson claimed that he never killed a white man."

The 1969 introduction to *Crow Killer*, by Richard Dorson of the American Folklore Society, does admit that "tribal narrations" would likely have cast Johnston as "a demon-possessed white ogre."

It turns out the book, including its supposed scholarship and the revenge tale, is a big load of malarkey, a point made repeatedly in the first real biography of Johnston, *Avenging Fury of the Plains: Exploding the Myths, Discovering the Man* by Dennis John McLelland, which first appeared in 2008. Unfortunately, McLelland's book is flawed and far from a definitive case, further muddying Johnston scholarship.

John "Liver-Eating" Johnston never ate *anyone's* liver," McLelland writes. Instead, the nickname was permanently attached to him during a retaliatory battle with the Sioux (not the Crows) in 1868. Johnston stabbed a Sioux warrior then withdrew his knife with a piece of the unfortunate's liver attached. Covered in blood from the fight, he offered the snack to recoiling associates then pretended to eat it himself.

The truth is probably some variation of that. A bloodier version has Johnston and some companions boiling the bodies of dead Indians to sell the skulls to tourists. When one was found still alive, the knife came out. Whatever actually happened, an indelible legend was born. Is it too much of a stretch to compare this stunt with Ozzy Osbourne of Black Sabbath biting the head off a live bat (he thought it was rubber) in 1982? That move made a career, too.

Nathan E. Bender, in a new introduction to a 2016 edition of *Crow Killer*, gives credit to McLelland for "enthusiastically" pointing out the earlier book's historical inaccuracies. He writes that *Crow Killer* is not even correctly described as historical fiction, because most writers of such material base their creations on actual people and events. "Instead," says Bender, "Thorp and Bunker intentionally created a mythic American saga under the guise of passing on legitimate oral traditions of a historical frontiersman."

Bender told me that Bunker admitted to him in a letter that he'd made up many elements of the story as part of a "reimagining" of the book's plot. That may have included adding the wife/revenge angle. Johnston himself only ever said he had a beef with the Crows for stealing his furs, and in letters to Montana newspapers he denied ever having been married to anyone. "But the book's version is more romantic, and gives the reader more sympathy for Johnston," Bender said.

The Crows didn't depict Johnston as a demon-possessed ogre; in fact, the tribe today considers Johnston to have been friendly to them. Chief Joseph Medicine Crow, a tribal elder, told Bender that Johnston would eat raw deer liver with them—perhaps that's where the nickname comes from.

In later life, Johnston would do his liver-eating act on stage. (Collection number 943-008, Montana Historical Society Research Center Photograph Archives, Helena, MT)

It's not surprising that the real John Johnston can't live up to his legend, and is described by those who knew him as a quick-tempered man of little distinction, albeit with some minor accomplishments as a scout, trapper, and constable. Author Robert Utley in *A Life Wild and Perilous* says Johnston was "an unlearned, unwashed, drunk, and violent . . . [frontiersman] who tore a bloody swatch across the then-unconquered American West."

Just how bloody the swath was depends on who's talking. Johnston very much wanted to be seen as an Indian killer (though in his telling the victims were Sioux and Blackfeet, and only a few Crows), and so had a major role in burnishing his own legend. Bender concludes that *Crow Killer* may have been "fatally flawed," but the romantic story it told hit a nerve and became "a fixture in modern popular culture." And Robert Redford's *Jeremiah Johnson* added its own aura.

Bender told me in an interview, "The strength of the story overrode the historical validity. People wanted it to be true. It took more than thirty years before historians woke up."

So, in 1861, did Johnston really get captured by Blackfeet and tied to a stake, only to chew through his rawhide bindings, kill and scalp his guard, then make off with the man's leg—which sustained him while he made his way home (two hundred miles in the dead of winter)? Probably not—though it's reported in *Crow Killer* and a variation may have actually happened to an undoubtedly fearsome and murderous cannibalistic mountain man named Levi Boone Helm (the leg reportedly belonged to his dead white companion). But maybe Johnston told the story about himself, possibly adding the detail that he'd also used the leg to fend off a mountain lion.

It's altogether fitting that near the end of his days, in 1884, Johnston ate (or pretended to eat) livers for a paying public in a traveling show, with Calamity Jane no less, designed to cash in on the profits made by Buffalo Bill Cody. The Indian actors were Crows, who apparently bore him no ill will. After all, they were (mostly) Johnston's victims only in a fictional account.

WHAT WE ACTUALLY KNOW

The record of Johnston's early years is sparse, though we know that he was born in 1824. His original family name is unclear, but it may have been Garrison, and his father's name was Isaac. He came into this world not in Montana or Wyoming but in the (then) far more placid Little York, New Jersey. Some sources say Johnston had five sisters, one of whom lived until 1923.

McLelland writes that Johnston's father treated him brutally, and perhaps that was a factor in his running away to join the navy—as John Garrison. This is where Johnston's record as a hothead originates, because he reportedly lasted only five days. McLelland told the *Los Angeles Times*, "He deserted the Navy after he struck an officer, and changed his name to John Johnston."

A vivid and somewhat fanciful biography at JohnLiverEatingJohnston.com adds this detail, based closely on a 1900 obituary in the *Carbon County Democrat*:

> When the Lieutenant in charge struck one of his comrades with a sword, Johnston, in a fit of rage, struck him in the neck, which laid him out senseless on the deck of the ship. When the Lieutenant came to, he didn't know whether lightning or a spar had hit him, but he thought it was Johnston. . . . When he finally was allowed to go ashore, he never came back and ventured off into the unknown west.

On the run from the military, Johnston found work as a "woodhawk" supplying firewood to steamers along the Missouri, and also mined for gold in Montana and California. It's not known how long Johnston stayed in gold country, but he was definitely in Montana by 1860.

By the time Johnston arrived in Montana, the beaver had been mostly hunted out, and fashions had changed from beaver hats anyway. But buffalo was in demand for buffalo robes, and Johnston found work supplying food for the army (as Buffalo Bill did for the railroad crews).

Johnston's legend makes much of his fearsome sixteen-pound Sharps buffalo rifle, which McLelland says was a "needle gun," shooting a spike-shaped bullet that would stop anything in its path. He also reportedly carried a twelve-inch Bowie knife, a Colt pistol, and a hand-carved tomahawk. Familiarity with the terrain and being handy with weaponry undoubtedly helped Johnston when during the Civil War in 1864 he signed on for a three-year stint with the Union's Second Colorado Cavalry as a "veteran recruit" (and scout after June of 1864).

Hugh Lenox Scott's 1928 *Some Memories of a Soldier* (later retitled *Sign Talker*) has a fine reminiscence about Johnston's scouting days that reinforces his reputation as a teller of tall tales. "At night we would all gather around a huge fire and listen to stories from the scouts, mainly from Liver-Eating [John] Johnson, who was said to have eaten a piece of an Indian's liver in a fit of bravado," Scott wrote. "His language was very quaint, and we would often listen to him until one o'clock in the morning. He was a tall, powerful man with a hairy torso like that of a bull. He carried a 16-pound buffalo Sharps rifle, which, with its belt full of ammunition, was a load for an ordinary man."

Killing antelope was part of Johnston's duties, and he would return to camp with two, one under each arm. But Scott also writes that when the liver eater left the army camp "a bunch of our horses left the same night."

Johnston also served under General Miles with the frontier scout Yellowstone Kelly, who described him in his memoirs as "the celebrated hunter and frontiersman."

In 1865, Johnston mustered out and returned to Montana. McLelland says he had served "with both distinction and dishonor," evidently spending much of the war not fighting but serving as a spy from a base in a Confederate unit. In 1869, he was reportedly in Canada helping run a "whiskey fort" on the Highwood River, in Whoop-Up country, after the British administration was withdrawn. Johnston was suspected of supplying the local Blackfeet with blankets infected with smallpox—revenge for horse theft.

During the Indian wars of 1876 to 1877, Johnston scouted for General Samuel Sturgis, and for General Nelson A. Miles, who "gathered around him a band of old-time frontiersmen." McLelland says Johnston "did play a role (albeit, a minor one) in the opening of the American west."

The chronology of events in Johnston's life are more than a little muddled. *Crow Killer* maintains that Johnston came under the tutelage of "remarkable men in their chosen field" with names like "Bear Claw" Chris Lapp, "Del" Gue, Old John Hatcher (who taught him scalping techniques), and Bill Williams, and proved an apt pupil. Some of these people may never have existed, but Del Gue shows up as a character in *Jeremiah Johnson*, proclaiming,

> These here is God's finest sculpturing! [pointing to the Rocky Mountains]. And there ain't no laws for the brave ones! And there ain't no asylums for the crazy ones! And there ain't no churches except for this right here! And there ain't no priests excepting the birds! By God, I are a mountain man, and I'll live until an arrow or a bullet finds me!

And it was in May of 1847, *Crow Killer* reports, that "Crow Indians killed and scalped John Johnston's pregnant wife; for many years thereafter, he killed and scalped Crow Indians. Then he ate their livers, raw. He ate them not for hunger's sake, but upon principle. . . ."

Bender said there's no record of Johnston on the frontier until 1860, so he could not have had a pregnant Flathead Indian wife in 1847. But *Crow Killer* goes into detail about that wife, whom he supposedly bought from her father, a subchief named Bear's Head. The price was a rifle (surely not a Sharps?), two knives, and a supply of salt and sugar.

"The girl was known as The Swan," *Crow Killer* says, "perhaps because her head had been allowed to grow with natural curve; through some oversight, her mother had neglected to fasten the usual flat rock to her skull." She was supposedly the daughter of a Flathead subchief, and Johnston (then only nineteen) purchased her from her father. Del Gue is credited with the information that "she was comely." The Swan became pregnant, Johnston went out tending his traplines, and when he came back she'd been slaughtered by the Crows. Thus, a one-man war began.

In general, though, the Crows (although warlike with other tribes) had amicable relations with whites, and were close to the army. A scout's wife would, then, seem an unlikely target. But I couldn't find any mention of a Del Gue (sometimes written as Del Que) in contemporary historical records, save in the memoirs of another *Crow Killer* informant, John "White Eye" Anderson. And Johnston, in a letter to the Billings newspaper in 1884, denied he ever "kept a squaw as a wife," calling any statement to the contrary "a malicious falsehood."

Dates for the supposed liver-eating years vary wildly, from the late 1840s to between 1868 and 1870. In 1869, Johnston was reported to have installed rows of grinning Indian skulls on riverbank stakes for passing steamboat passengers to enjoy.

But when asked about eating human livers later in life, Johnston typically retorted that the story was "a joke." In an 1868 letter to a Montana newspaper, the man himself said it was all a misunderstanding. He had merely offered a friend a piece of liver from an Indian he killed. "He refused," Johnston wrote, "but told everyone he seen me eating the Indian liver. But I don't eat any . . . just rubbed it over my mouth to make the man think I was eating it."

Contemporary accounts of Johnston's liver eating really go over the top, though. In one, he took a Crow corpse and "mutilated it with his teeth in the most shocking manner, and drank the blood as it flowed trickling from his victim." In a version of the naming story, he cut out the liver while the poor unfortunate was still alive.

Accounts of the 1884 tour with Calamity Jane make good reading. According to James D. McLaird's *Calamity Jane: The Woman, the Legend*, the Hardwick "Great Rocky Mountain Show" had competition from concurrent shows led by Sitting Bull, Buffalo Bill, Pawnee Bill, and many others—there were as many as fifty western extravaganzas—and that's one reason it failed to prosper. The show must have been an expensive proposition to keep on the road, featuring as it did one hundred Indians, cowboys, and animals.

Johnston's cabin in Red Lodge, Montana. (Wikipedia)

The star was not Johnston, who reenacted his liver eating and served as manager of no less than forty Crows (ten of them women), but Curley, an Indian scout described as the only survivor of Custer's troop, who became very famous. Bender writes that Johnston "apparently had at least some natural ability as an actor," and was "consciously portraying himself as a heroic figure to a paying audience."

Calamity Jane, who was late joining the troupe, was reported in the *Billings Post* as "erratic" and "not so attractive in appearance as she was in the early days of Deadwood." Despite Johnston's work keeping them together, several of the Crows defected from the company to head back to Montana. That must have been a blow, because the promoters were getting ten cents a throw for off-show visits to the "Indian camp."

The show reached Milwaukee, where a reporter described a stylized Indian attack on an emigrant train and stagecoach. "When the red devils bound their unfortunate captives to the

The Indian scout Curley, supposedly the only member of Custer's troop to survive the massacre, became the star of a Wild West show, upstaging "Liver-Eating" Johnston. D.F. Barry cabinet card, circa 1885. (Wikipedia)

stake, preparatory to burning them alive, the excitement of the vast crowd became intense, and when the daring scouts came gallantly to the rescue, dispersing the Indians and releasing the captives they were greeted with a round of applause."

After touring for the summer, the company, having been paid mostly in promises, dissolved in August. And "the portly form of John Johnson" was again seen on the streets of Billings, Montana, proclaiming he was going to do another show—with himself as star. The Livingston newspaper reported that he "had a good time" on his theatrical foray. The remaining Crows reportedly had to sell their ponies to get back to Big Sky Country.

Johnson wasn't finished yet—he had a long, documented stint as a constable in Red Lodge, Montana, and was celebrated for providing local color there. And he was still

An early depiction of cannibalism in the New World. A 1505 account from the voyage of Amerigo Vespucci contained an image of a man on a spit. (Wikipedia)

CANNIBALISM IN AMERICA

The grisly story of the Donner Party (perhaps led astray by Louis Vasquez and Jim Bridger) is well-known, but have there been other instances of cannibalism in the Americas, even in the pre-Columbian period?

Sure. Looking beyond the Aztecs, who were believed to practice ritual cannibalism (though not as a regular part of their diet), there's some evidence that it also occurred among the native peoples of the Southwest. After considering the evidence (high percentage of broken bones in samples, anvil abrasions, cut marks, missing bones), scholar Toni Gore, writing in *Popular Archaeology*, concludes: "After considering alternative explanations for the presence of severely damaged disarticulated human remains in the American Southwest, including the use of secondary burials, extreme violence as a means of social control, and the execution of witches, archaeological evidence demonstrates that the presence of these remains can only be accounted for by the occurrence of cannibalistic activities in the region." Wow.

Not to get too gory here, but a study from 2000 of cannibalism in the Mesa Verde region cites as principal evidence "a tool kit associated with the processing of human remains. The kit included two flakes, a large chopper, a chopper-like cobble tool and two ground axes. The results of blood residue analysis conducted on this tool kit revealed human blood residue on two of the flakes."

Other possible explanations for these discoveries include a ritual punishment of suspected witches, or the possibility that "severe acts of bodily mutilation were undertaken as an act of social control."

Early explorers saw cannibalism everywhere. Amerigo Vespucci, who lent his name to our country, said of the native people he saw in Brazil, "They also eat each other even those who are slain, and hang the flesh of them in the smoke." He added, in a blow to credibility, "They become 150 years old. And have no government."

Let's not forget the more modern cannibals. Alfred Packer was a prospector who admitted he'd committed cannibalism in the mountains of Colorado during the cold winter of 1874. He and five others were snowbound, and Packer—the only one still alive—admitted to living off the flesh of his companions. After being sentenced to death, he was retried and got forty years for manslaughter. *Cannibal! The Musical* is based on Packer's story.

Mountain man Levi Boone Helm was famous as "The Kentucky Cannibal," and reportedly ate the flesh of several people between 1850 and 1854. Helm, also a murderer and thief (as well as a confirmed Confederate) said, "Many's the poor devil I've killed, at one time or another . . . and the time has been that I've been obliged to feed on some of 'em." Helm, who was ultimately executed for his crimes, is the probable origin of the legend—associated with "Liver-Eating" Johnston—of a mountain man living off a companion's leg on a difficult trek.

feisty. According to an 1886 report by S. P. Panton in the *Billings Gazette*, when Johnston was sixty-two he was challenged to take on a professional fighter behind the saloon. "Johnson saw no need for gloves," the story says. "His first blow sent the professional boxer through a board fence, and his second blow convinced the fighter that he wasn't in the same class as Johnson."

Panton also reports on the origins of the liver eating, adding the detail that the Indian may or may not have been dead when his

Johnston's grave makes clear the "Jeremiah Johnson" connection. (Wikipedia)

organ was cut out, and quoting Johnston as saying, "Who would take his liver rare?" But Panton can't confirm that any liver was actually eaten.

After a failed attempt to raise cabbages on a Yellowstone River island, Johnston built a cabin near the stage station at Red Lodge, where in 1895 he became the town's first constable. A colorful and perhaps fanciful obituary in the *Fergus County Argus* from February 14, 1900, relates that Johnston had earlier been a deputy sheriff in Custer County, and was serving there in the 1880s when his "bosom companion," a fellow lawman named "Muggins" Taylor, "was shot and killed in the discharge of his duties by Henry Lump, a drunken galoot whose wife supported him by taking in washing."

The hand-hewn log cottage Johnston built in Red Lodge survives (although moved to a new location), and has a short front door and ceilings low enough to call into question the "fact" that Johnston was at least six feet tall. Legends tend to grow in stature—some sources say Johnston was six feet six.

Johnston's last few days were spent far from the frontier, in sunny Santa Monica, California. In 1899 or 1900, penniless, he washed up at the Old Soldiers home there, and was buried in a military cemetery near the San Diego Freeway.

The *Argus* obituary reports Johnston did not leave Red Lodge for California willingly, but physical and financial reality left him with little choice. "Upon leaving Red Lodge less than two months ago," it said, "the old man broke down and wept like a child as the train whirled him away from his friends, and it is fair to presume that his last thoughts as he lay dying in a strange land, among strange people in that home by the side of the sea, were of those generous friends and exciting scenes of former days."

Johnston was later to be dug up from California in 1974, following a campaign by some middle-school students who'd formed a "Committee for the Reburial of Liver-Eating Johnston" the year before.

The old scout was then moved to Old Trail Town in Cody, Wyoming, where the grave site (adorned with a bronze equestrian statue) is a tourist attraction. More than two thousand people attended the reinterment, probably the largest burial service ever in Wyoming. Robert Redford was one of the pallbearers, and the only one who didn't think it fitting to dress in frontier gear. In fact, he looked totally Hollywood.

The stone, in a nod to the movie, says "John 'Jeremiah Liver-Eating' Johnson." There were even newspaper reports that "Jeremiah Johnson" was being reburied. It's ironic that Johnston ended up in Buffalo Bill's town, because the two hated each other, and according to Montana congressman John Melcher, once engaged in fisticuffs. "At Johnston's funeral," Bender told me, "people who should have known better—local historians—were calling him Jeremiah Johnson."

When Bender conducted a survey of visitors to Johnston's grave in Cody, sixty-five percent of those asked about the man buried there gave details from the *Jeremiah Johnson* film. Only fifteen percent knew about the real man from books.

WHAT HE SAID

From *Crow Killer*: "He never attempted to dodge a difficult situation, yet he never sought an encounter or ignored one in his reckoning. His trade was trapping; the mountains were his home; and the killing of those who would disrupt either became, for one with his skills, merely routine."

The *Billings Gazette* quotes a ready-for-retirement Johnston as saying, "I'll go and build me a cabin in the mountains where I can kill all I want and I'll never work again."

HUGH GLASS

THE ELUSIVE

REVENANT

HUGH GLASS

It is generally agreed that Hugh Glass had a near-fatal encounter with a bear, but after that accounts differ. (Wikipedia)

THE LEGEND

Hugh Glass was a beaver trapper and mountain man in the early days of western exploration, the 1820s and 1830s, when game was still plentiful. He had a Pawnee wife and a half-Pawnee son, Hawk, but though Glass tried to save her, his wife was killed in a raid by soldiers.

In March of 1823, Glass (accompanied by the surviving Hawk) left St. Louis on his first trip up the Missouri River, signing on with a famous fur-trading expedition led by Andrew Henry and William Ashley.

He'd answered an ad in the *Missouri Republican* calling for one hundred mountaineers to join the trip. The company's mountain men included Jim Bridger, James Clyman, Jedediah Smith, and William Sublette.

Several months later, the expedition was attacked by Arikara Indians (looking for the chief's daughter, Powaqa, taken by white men), and Glass barely escaped alive. One trapper, John Fitzgerald, harbored a deep hatred of Indians and taunted Hawk, but his father intervened to prevent a confrontation.

An excellent marksman, and benefiting from the skills he learned from the Pawnees, Glass was often charged with scouting, as well as hunting and gathering for the group. Later that summer, he was out looking for game (near what is now Lemmon, South Dakota), and he was attacked by a bear. He initially fended it off, but it attacked and mauled him again. Although he finally drew his knife and killed the mother bear—

which fell on top of him—Glass was severely wounded, with a broken leg, a punctured throat, a ripped scalp, and multiple deep gashes.

Glass's fellow trappers found him, grievously wounded, and unlikely to survive. Henry offered seventy-five dollars to anyone who would stay with Glass until he died, and two men, John Fitzgerald and young Jim Bridger, were chosen. Fitzgerald, who was worried that Indians would attack if they remained with Glass, tried to smother the wounded man while Bridger was absent, but Hawk, coming upon this scene, tried to stop him. In a melee, Hawk was killed.

When Bridger (who hid Hawk's body) returned, Fitzgerald convinced him to abandon Glass, and together they took everything that Glass needed to survive, including his gun, knife, and food. Miraculously, Glass—aided by a fortuitous encounter with the Pawnee, survived. He repaid the Pawnee by rescuing Powaqa from French trappers. A stronger Glass made his way some two hundred miles to Fort Kiowa. He forgave Bridger, who he discovered was only following orders.

Glass continued to track Fitzgerald, and there was an epic battle by a river. Fitzgerald blurted out that killing him won't bring Hawk back. At this point, the Pawnee band, reunited with Powaqa, arrived at the river. Glass pushed a wounded Fitzgerald into the river, and it's the Indian chief who actually killed Glass's nemesis.

Glass was spared by the Pawnees, because he rescued Powaqa. He went on to many other trapping adventures, sustained by the memory of his Native American wife and son.

HOW THEY GET IT WRONG

The account on the previous pages is, of course, nonsense, but mostly follows the plot of *The Revenant*, a recent film dramatization of Glass's life starring Leonardo DiCaprio. Although the bear attack in the movie is fairly faithful to what happened to Glass in real life, the subplot involving Glass's Indian family (and semi-mystical encounters) is wholly grafted onto the story.

The Indian attack seen in the film actually happened—it left thirteen to fifteen of the company's men dead—but Indian princesses weren't involved.

There are strong parallels between Hugh Glass/*The Revenant* and John "Liver-Eating" Johnston/*Jeremiah Johnson*. In both films, the real people are given Native American wives and children to both humanize (or spiritualize) them and give them a motivation for revenge.

The irony here is that the story of Hugh Glass is actually fairly clear in the historical record. He was a trapper, he got mauled by a bear, and he survived. In real life, there were no revenge killings. Bridger was forgiven. Fitzgerald had become a soldier, and thus was protected, though Glass did get his gun back.

In fact, there's no evidence that Glass had a Native American family, though he did spend time with the Pawnees. He stayed in the wilderness, resumed trapping, and was killed in an encounter with the Arikaras some years later. Because he didn't live to give interviews or write a book, there's no story that got wildly embroidered in the telling. Glass remains a rather mysterious figure, and there were remarkably few tall tales surrounding him—at least until Tinseltown found the story.

The Revenant, based on the harrowing novel by Michael Punke, is actually the second film about Hugh Glass and the bear attack. The first—1971's *Man in the Wilderness*, starring Richard Harris and John Huston—also grafts on some Native American mumbo jumbo.

Director Alejandro González Iñárritu's *Revenant* is "based in part on the novel by Michael Punke." The disclaimer was necessary because the movie takes such liberty with the Hawk-and-wife-free book. In fact, Iñárritu and co-writer Mark L. Smith make the exact same choices the makers of *Jeremiah Johnson* and the writers of *Crow Killer* did—the Indian angle adds spiritual depth, and the dead wives amp up the revenge motivation.

Jacob Hall, writing in *Screen Crush*, gets it right.

> The messy murkiness of the novel, where the reasons for Glass's revenge are so low key and personal and downright *strange*, is haunting because it forces the reader to connect with a hero whose mission seems so extreme. By tossing in that plot device of a son, Iñárritu and Smith have taken the easy way out. For a movie that is otherwise unafraid of being as off-putting, intense, and brutal as possible, it's such an odd choice. It's such a *Hollywood* choice.

And this is a Hollywood movie, not a European art film with an ambiguous ending.

Hugh Glass, a man of incomparable grit. But there's no evidence of an Indian son. (Wikipedia)

WHAT WE ACTUALLY KNOW

Not much is definitively known about Hugh Glass before 1823. He was just one more trapper in a wilderness that offered them a chance to make a living. The website HughGlass.org speculates that he was born somewhere near Philadelphia around 1783. Much of what we know after that is through a fellow trapper named George C. Yount, who claimed to have been a friend of the generally solitary Glass.

Yount told his story to Reverend Orange Clark, who compiled notes that were edited in 1923 by historian Charles Lewis Camp for publication in the *California Historical Society Quarterly*. In *The Saga of Hugh Glass: Pirate, Pawnee, and Mountain Man* by John Myers Myers, the author complains that Reverend Clark "obviously didn't know how to draw his subject out, nor did his ignorance of the West and its leading personalities allow him to ask enough of the right questions when Yount proffered a likely topic."

Nevertheless, Yount described Glass as "bold, daring, reckless & excentric [*sic*] to a high degree." But he added that Glass "was nevertheless a man of great talents & intellectual as well as bodily power." The quality that stood out was "bravery."

According to Yount, Glass "first commenced life in the capacity of a sailor" (another parallel to "Liver-Eating" Johnston). Supposedly, he was captured by a "desperate band of Pirates under the notorious [Jean] Lafitte." It was become a pirate or die, and Glass took the oath, suffering through "the cruel murders to be perpetuated daily."

Off the coast of Texas, Glass and a companion were deemed unfit pirates, but escaped the night before they were to be executed. The two wandered the trackless wilderness then were taken prisoner again, this time by the Pawnee.

Once more, they were to be executed at the stake, this time. Glass's companion indeed died a horrible death, but because Glass produced a large packet of vermillion, prized by the Pawnee, and offered it to the chief along with a bow, he was spared. After that, Glass got nothing but "paternal & tender treatment" from the Indians. It is said he learned navigation (without a compass), tracking and survival skills from them. In 1822, the tribe traveled to St. Louis and Glass took the opportunity to escape from them (without a wife and child). The trip with Ashley happened eight to ten months later.

Yount's story has more than a little Robert Louis Stevenson to it, and who knows if Glass was ever a sailor, or captured by pirates. Still, Yount's account of the bear mauling is remarkably faithful to other versions, right down to description of the wounds, and the two (unidentified) men leaving him for dead after taking his worldly goods. The amount they were to be paid, he said, was "four hundred Dolls"—an enormous sum at the time.

Glass's story was first made public in 1825, just two years after the events in question. It appears in the *Port Folio*, published in Philadelphia and entitled "Letters From the West: The Missouri Trapper." The unnamed author writes that he heard the story from Glass directly at Fort Atkinson on the Upper Missouri "in June last." He adds, "Whether old Ireland, or Scotch-Irish Pennsylvania, claims the honour of his nativity, I have not ascertained with precision."

His skill with a rifle much esteemed, Glass was on a hunting party in a thicket when attacked by a "white bear" (actually a grizzly) that was looking to feed her cubs. Glass managed to escape and give his foe a mortal shot. Glass is quoted: "I burst the varment [*sic*]."

An account taken from the diary of expedition member James Clyman (who got it secondhand) says that before the mauling Glass fired a shot at the bear, which hit home but only seemed to enrage the animal. Glass tried to escape by climbing a tree, but the bear pulled him down and did grievous damage. Members of the party arrived and shot the bear, but it was still alive—and attacked Glass a second time. This version is followed fairly closely by *Man in the Wilderness*, but in *The Revenant* it's Glass who kills the bear—with a knife.

Glass had sustained "several dangerous wounds," *Port Folio* reports, and was unable to travel. Again, two members of the party were offered a reward, they stayed with Glass five days then the "unprincipled wretches" (unnamed) left him to his fate after taking his weapons.

"Glass rose from his grave and walked into the history books," reported *True West* magazine. Most accounts say the mountain man survived mostly due to the strength of his iron will, though *Port Folio* said a friendly group of Mandans offered last-minute assistance getting safely to the nearest fort. *The Revenant* film exaggerates the Native American help.

During his ordeal, Glass, often crawling, initially made a miserable two miles a day. He lived on berries until he had the good fortune to encounter some wolves with a young buffalo kill—a scene depicted in the film. He chased away the wolves and ate the fatted calf, evidently raw because the wretches had taken his flint.

Meanwhile, the trapper principally responsible for leaving Glass had moved on to Fort Atkinson, and so Glass set off in pursuit, barely recovered, on February 29, 1824—in the dead of winter. On the way, Glass and his companions were waylaid by a band of Arikaras who at first appeared to be friendly then stole the trappers' goods. Glass barely escaped with his life, but two of his fellow travelers were killed.

Now with a knife, flint, and steel—"little fixens" that "make a man feel righ peart when he is three or four hundred miles *from any body* or *any place*"—Glass finally makes it to Fort Atkinson and Council Bluffs. There, according to *Port Folio*, he "found his old traitorous acquaintance in the garb of a private soldier. This shielded the delinquent from chastisement." The post's commanding officer orders the soldier (presumably Fitzgerald) to return the rifle and other goods. "This appeased the wrath of Hugh Glass," the narrative concludes.

This version probably has some resemblance to what actually happened, though details vary considerably. In 1839, the story was added to by Kentucky writer Edmund

Opposite: "A rough and tumble with a grizzley." Such encounters were common on the frontier. (Wikipedia)

A grizzly bear family in Glacier National Park. (Wikipedia)

WHEN A BEAR ATTACKS

The website Blackbearheaven.com has many accounts of fatal black and grizzly bear attacks from 2010 to today in Alaska and the lower forty-eight. Some victims apparently made fatal mistakes in thinking that the bears they encountered were benign.

Forty-nine-year-old Richard White was killed in Alaska's Denali National Park in 2012 after taking close-up photographs of the apparently tranquil grizzly bear that then turned on him. And Timothy Treadwell and his girlfriend Amie Huguenard were also killed by a grizzly in 2003. As depicted in the brilliant Werner Herzog documentary *Grizzly Man*, Treadwell had lived among the grizzlies for thirteen summers, and apparently concluded they were his friends. He walked among them, even touched them, and it was okay until it wasn't.

According to Montana Fish, Wildlife, and Parks, when encountering a bear your first step is to decide if it's on the defense or the offense. An agitated bear will pin its ears back, lower its head, paw the ground, make woofing or growling sounds—or simply charge without warning.

"If a bear looks you directly in the eye with its ears back, it's definitely feeling threatened, and you should take this as a serious warning," reports HowStuffWorks. "If it begins to 'pop' its jaw, it's getting ready to charge."

A charging bear is pretty scary, but some charges are actually bluffs. If a bear charges and then stops, slowly back away. If it attacks and keeps coming, it's time for the pepper spray. If that doesn't work, your choices are to either play dead or get aggressive yourself. Good luck!

Flagg, who published "Adventures at the Headwaters of the Missouri" in the *Louisville Literary News Letter*. This account says that the Henry & Ashley expedition included 160 men, with two keelboats, and set off in March of 1822.

The group split up, and a small expedition under Henry's command set off with three loaded horses. Glass and another man, George Harris, went off in search of wild fruit. Harris heard some desperate cries and suspected an Indian attack, but he instead came upon Glass bleeding from at least fifteen bear wounds, "any one of which under ordinary circumstances would have been mortal."

A version in the *Southern Literary Messenger* from 1842 differs from *Port Folio* in some respects. It claims that Glass's hunting companions also saw the bear, but were further away from it, and "profited from their more favorable situation to attempt escape by flight, leaving [Glass] to his destiny." And the amount offered to stay with Glass is eighty dollars.

Flagg identifies the first man to stay behind as Fitzgerald and the second as "Bridges," later determined to be a young Jim Bridger. When they return to their company, they say that Glass had died of his wounds after six days. Fitzgerald gets his reward, in this case three hundred dollars.

Imagine everyone's surprise, then, when Glass shows up alive. Bridges/Bridger, the narrative said, "could with difficulty be persuaded to enter his presence," but Glass, finding him repentant, forgave him his crimes. Glass told his story to an awed audience, including that he was left for dead, but found a small brass kettle, a shot pouch, and a bit of dried buffalo beef, which sustained him for several days. Again, he comes upon the wolves and buffalo calf, and gains succor.

Here we get the detail that Glass was lucky enough to run into a friendly band of Sioux Indians, who treat him kindly and grant him safe passage to a French trading post. The *Messenger* version also includes the lucky encounter with the Sioux, who "acted toward him the part of the good Samaritan." Glass's wound was "full of worms," which the Sioux cleaned out with an astringent vegetable liquid.

"What an undertaking!" Flagg wrote. He details more of Glass's adventures, which include some hair-breadth escapes from the Indians, and then expresses amazement that the trapper would have endured so many hardships and still retain his "almost insane attachment to savage life."

And that's the truth of the matter. Glass continued to live on the edge. In the mid-1820s, his trapping party was attacked by a Shoshone band, and an arrowhead became lodged in his back. He had to hike out seven hundred miles to Taos, New Mexico, before it could be removed with a straight razor by another mountain man. But Glass once again recovered and was soon off again, looking for beaver around the Yellowstone River.

Prince Maximillian of Wied carried evidence of Glass' demise. (Wikipedia)

The end may have been inevitable, given Glass's dangerous lifestyle. Between 1832 and 1834, Alexander Phillip Maximillian, prince of Wied, made a pilgrimage to the new United States, and wrote about his adventures in the 1843 *Travels in the Interior of North America*. During a stay at Fort Union, he obtains a manuscript "respecting the life of Glass, the beaver hunter." It was "written down from his own words a short time before he was shot, with two of his companions [Edward Rose and Hilain Menard], by the Arikaras."

The fatal attack, which left the three mountain men scalped and plundered (with Glass's famous rifle among the booty) reportedly occurred in the spring of 1833, near Fort Cass in what is now Treasure County, Montana. James Beckwourth—who did have a genius for being where the action was—claimed to have been at Fort Cass then, and found the bodies lying on the ice. But, as with many Beckwourth tales, it's unlikely.

The prince reports that, soon after Glass was killed, a "man of the name of Gardner [Johnson Gardner, a fellow trapper and friend of Glass], who afterwards happened to meet with these Indians, killed two of them with his own hand, and I received the scalp of one of them, as a present, during my stay in the fort." Did this grisly souvenir make it back to the palaces of Europe?

The prince lived to write his book, but Gardner was killed soon after in another encounter with the Arikaras. Flagg adds the detail that Gardner had the two Indians he captured for killing Glass burned alive after they were scalped. Flagg said that Glass had apparently fallen victim "after a hundred escapes and warnings, to his own wild temerity."

Ultimately, the story of Hugh Glass has plenty of bravery, a lot of savagery, and near-miraculous escapes. It sets new standards for human endurance—trumping John Colter, whom we'll soon meet—but maybe a thimbleful of cross-cultural uplift. *The Revenant* film is exciting, but what actually happened is even more fascinating and inspiring.

WHAT HE SAID

The *Southern Literary Messenger* records the final reunion of Glass and the young man who deserted him, presumably Bridger. The latter "stood without power of any motion; his eyes rolled wildly in their sockets; his teeth chattered with fear, and a clammy sweat rose upon his ashy features." Glass addresses him in dialogue considerably at odds with the more folksy speech attributed to him at other times:

> Young man, it is Glass that is before you; the same that not content
> with leaving, you thought, to a cruel death upon the prairie, you robbed,
> helpless as he was, of his rifle, his knife, of all, with which he could hope
> to defend, or save himself from famishing in the desert. . . . I swore an
> oath that I would be revenged on you, and the wretch who was with you,
> and I ever thought to have kept it. . . . But I cannot take your life; I see
> you repent; you have nothing to fear from me; go—you are free—for
> your youth I forgive you.

After the Arikara attack, in which Glass was wounded in the leg, he was deputized to write a letter to the family of one of the deceased mountain men, John Gardiner. "My painfull duty it is to tell you of the deth of yr son wh befell at the hands of the Indians 2d June in the early morning," Glass wrote. "His things we will send to you. The savages are greatly treacherous."

Jedidiah Smith was an abstemious frontiersman and trapper who was also a mapmaker and an early Rocky Mountains explorer. And a friend of Mike Fink? Could be. (Wikipedia)

BEAR SURVIVORS

The much-traveled mountain man Jedediah Smith survived a vicious grizzly bear attack on an 1823 expedition into what is now South Dakota.

The bear emerged from a thicket and threw Smith to the ground, breaking ribs, tearing his ear off and ripping off his scalp. A companion named Jim Clyman sewed him back together, and after a ten-day recuperation Smith was again leading the trip. Courtesy of *National Geographic*, here are some more contemporary bear survival stories:

The late Jim Cole, a wildlife photographer and hiker, survived *twice* being badly hurt by grizzlies. He wore a pirate's patch over his left eye and had deep scratches on his face from those encounters. One of the bears bit his scalp and wrist, the other (fourteen years later) raked his face with her claws, taking out one eye. "How lucky I am," he said, "to still be ambulatory and in a place to bring more respect for the Great Bear."

In 2015, while hiking with her kids, fifty-two-year-old Laurie Cooksey was attacked and bitten by a black bear in Virginia's Douthat State Park. It was the first reported bear attack on a human in Virginia that was unrelated to hunting. Cooksey lived, after kicking the bear and persuading it to flee.

In 2013, sixty-five-year-old Nic Patrick of Cody, Wyoming, was mauled by a grizzly protecting her cubs on the Shoshone River. While he was being rushed to a hospital, he begged officials not to kill the bear—because it was just protecting its family.

In 2005, Johan Otter of Escondido, California, and his eighteen-year-old daughter, Jenna, barely survived a mother grizzly attack in Glacier National Park in Montana. Jenna had two bad bites, and she broke her back in two places. Otter was repeatedly attacked, and finally survived by playing dead. "About 60 percent of my head was 'de-gloved'—the bear essentially took my scalp off," he told *Backpacker*. "Its claw fractured my right eye socket and disrupted an eye muscle. One bite snapped my right wrist. I also broke my nose and two vertebrae; I had a compound fracture of my second cervical vertebra; I had bite wounds all over." He reports, "I don't find [bears] as cute as I used to."

JOHN "GRIZZLY" ADAMS

A WAY

WITH ANIMALS

GRIZZLY ADAMS

ADAMS AND BEN FRANKLIN.

THE LEGEND

Forced to live on the margins of society after being wrongfully accused of murder, James Capen "Grizzly" Adams built a cabin in the wilderness and, with his faithful companions Mad Jack, the Indian Nakoma, and a host of animals, including Ben, the bear cub he saved and raised, helped the people who visited the mountains. This onetime hunter and trapper resolved never to harm an animal unnecessarily.

Grizzly Adams with the redoubtable Ben Franklin.
(Towne & Bacon/Library of Congress)

HOW THEY GET IT WRONG

There actually was a bear named Ben, though his full name was Benjamin Franklin. John "Grizzly" Adams certainly looked the part of the nature-friendly mountain man, but that was mainly for the stage—he was (albeit briefly) a popular performer for P. T. Barnum. His actual time in the wilderness was brief, just three years, from 1853 to 1856.

The legend is largely based on the 1974 film *The Life and Times of Grizzly Adams*, which led to a TV series of the same name. *Gentle Ben* (TV show and movies) is the story in modern dress, with children added for cuteness—Ben Franklin lives! There's even a later 1999 movie called *Escape to Grizzly Mountain*, which denies any connection to the Grizzly Adams legend but follows it closely. And those stories were themselves based on fiction, a 1972 novella by Charles E. Sellier Jr.

The basic story is simple—and heart-warming. But it's far from the truth. Yes, there was a real "Grizzly" Adams, but his name was John, not James. And he did adopt a bear cub he named Ben, but he didn't risk his life to do it, and the cub only required rescuing because he'd killed its mother. Nobody accused Adams of murder, though he was certainly guilty of the slaughter of many animals.

Adams wasn't particularly civic minded, or at least that part of him didn't make it into the biography written during his lifetime. And it's purely ludicrous to think that he had any special affinity for the creatures of the forest, or that he'd swear an oath to never harm them unnecessarily—the real Adams was quite trigger-happy. And there was no great later-life awakening on that score.

But then, Grizzly Adams has always been more myth than man. During his lifetime, Adams's story was considerably enlarged upon by San Francisco newspaper journalist Theodore Hittell. The tale-spinning writer turned the mountain man into a legend in his own time with a series of articles and then a book, the 1860 *Adventures of James Capen Adams: Mountaineer and Grizzly Bear Hunter of California*. Note two things: Hittell got his subject's first name wrong, and showcased him (accurately) as a hunter, not as a gentle friend of all the animals.

The movie and TV show repeat the fiction that the Grizzly Man was named James Capen Adams.

By the way, the bear on California's state flag was actually modeled on a painting of one of the animals in Adams's menagerie, Samson—billed in his lifetime as "the largest grizzly bear ever caught."

An illustration from Grizzly Adams' autobiography. He was more into shooting bears than being their friends. (Library of Congress)

WHAT WE ACTUALLY KNOW

Biographer Hittell first encountered Grizzly Adams not in the woods but in the comfortable confines of San Francisco, where in 1856 his eyes were drawn to a placard announcing "The Mountaineer Museum" and an exotic collection of animals, including Samson, Ben Franklin, and Lady Washington—pacing restlessly on their chains.

And Adams, their keeper, of course. Hittell describes him as of medium size, muscular and wiry, with gray hair and a white beard. "He was dressed in coat and pantaloons of buckskin, fringed at the edges and along the seams of arms and legs. On his head he wore a cap of deerskin, ornamented with a foxtail, and on his feet, buckskin moccasins." In other words, the very picture of the mountain man.

Adams was said to have "perfect control" over his bears, and could get them to rear up on their hind legs, walk erect, growl on command, and mock-fight, both with him and with each other. They appeared to enjoy the sport. The bare patches on their backs, Adams said, were from being saddled as pack animals. To prove his point that he had trained beasts of burden, Adams rode Ben Franklin bareback around his basement exhibit space.

Adams kept his menagerie—which also included black bears, elk, cougars, and eagles—in San Francisco for several years. During that time, Hittell relates, "He continued to wear buckskin, and when seen on the street, it was almost always in his mountaineer garb. He slept, on a buffalo robe or bearskin, in one corner of his exhibition room or in a small adjoining chamber. He sometimes cooked his own meals, but usually dined at a restaurant." Around this time, the widely known western artist Charles Nahl painted Adams, with Ben at his side. He also did a great portrait of Samson, which was adapted for the state flag.

Adams wasn't good at saving money and so, in 1860, when the mountain man decamped with the collection to New York, "he was substantially as poor in purse as when he first came to San Francisco." But before Adams left, he told Hittell his life story.

"I told him plainly that I wanted nothing except the truth, and he assured me that he would give it," the author wrote.

John Adams grew up far from his beloved California, in Medway, Massachusetts. He came from an illustrious family, particularly so in Massachusetts, and was descended from John and John Quincy Adams, as well as the patriot Sam Adams.

The family name may have been golden, but young Adams had to work for a living—as a shoemaker, a trade he learned as a teenage apprentice. Adams's ability to tame wild animals was not immediately apparent, because his first attempt—with a Bengal tiger belonging to his employer, did not go well. It had become "refractory," Adams says in his biography.

The fearless young man, then twenty-one, entered the tiger's cage several times, and on the last occasion "the magnificent but treacherous beast struck me to the floor and buried his teeth and claws in my flesh." A long convalescence ensued, and Adams says it temporarily ended his career as a hunter.

Luckily, Adams's injuries did not prevent him from working with his hands, so he returned to shoemaking in Boston with renewed vigor, and over a period of fifteen years amassed a considerable fortune of six to eight thousand dollars. He also married, and with his wife, the former Cylena Drury, had three children, Arabella, Arathusa, and Seymour.

Adams—"Yankee that I was"—had an entrepreneurial spirit, and so took his money and invested in a cargo of shoes and boots, which he shipped to St. Louis, where he hoped the demand would allow him to double or treble his capital. Adams wasn't a lucky guy, however, and his entire stock was consumed in a fire. "In one short night, I found myself a ruined man," he said.

But gold fever was consuming the country, and thousands of people were descending on California. Adams, with no other prospects, decided to join them. After "numberless hardships and privations" (the details of which should have been in the book) he arrived in the Golden State by way of Mexico in the fall of 1849, minus Cylena and their children.

Instead of going back to shoemaking Adams tried trading, raising stock, and farming—doing well in some periods, poorly in others. He failed three different times, and by 1852 he was "disgusted with the world and dissatisfied with myself." And so he gave up his get-rich-quick schemes, turned his back on the society of his fellows, "and took the road toward the wildest and most unfrequented parts of the Sierra Nevada, resolved thenceforth to make the wilderness my home and wild beasts my companions."

And why not? Adams was in the prime of his life, and ready for adventure, and in short course he looked the part of the mountain man—complete with long gray hair and long gray beard and mustache.

Adams salvaged a meager stake from what remained of his estate—"an old wagon, two oxen, an old Kentucky rifle which used 30 balls to the pound of lead, a Tennessee rifle which used 60, a Colt revolving pistol, and several Bowie knives. Besides these, my effects were poor indeed,—a few tools, several pairs of blankets, a little clothing, and this was all."

The Eastern-bred tenderfoot could have been expected to fail in the mountains, but he didn't. He befriended the California Indians (numerous then, but almost gone by 1910), who appreciated his hunting and fishing skills, in turn making him a wigwam and several buckskin suits that he adopted as his costume in the woods. After the Indians moved down the mountain, Adams was alone for months at a time—and found himself enjoying "the happiness of a king."

Fate took a turn when Adams's brother, William, who had been in California for some time, discovered his sibling's hiding place in the mountains. At first he attempted to get Adams to come with him back to Massachusetts, and when that was unavailing, he hatched an alternative business partnership. Adams would capture some of California's abundant native fauna for exhibition purposes. They shook hands on the deal.

On a foraging trip down to Oregon and Washington, Adams and his party captured not only a pair of black bear cubs but (after killing their mother) another strapping pair of year-old grizzlies, one of whom became Adams's boon companion, Lady Washington.

"From that time to this," Adams said, "she has always been with me; and often has she shared my dangers and privations, borne my burdens, and partaken of my meals. The reader may be surprised to hear of a grizzly companion and friend; but Lady Washington has been both to me."

Grizzly Adams was hardly a great friend of the animals. His biography has page after page of killing rituals—antelopes, bears, wolves, buffalos—whatever came into his sights, including many, many bears, some of which he seems to have killed for no particular reason. Indeed, Adams was capable of rapturous descriptions of animals— like this elk—just before sending slugs into said beast.

> I discovered a band of five or six elks. There was one of them, a splendid buck, with fine antlers, and magnificent bearing, which particularly attracted my attention. Could he have been transported, as he stood there, into the midst of the world, poets and painters would have paid tribute to his beauty; no stag of Landseer has a nobler mien, or more of the spirit of freedom in his limbs.

Adams tended to ascribe human motivations to animals who were, after all, just doing what came naturally. He referred to a prowling panther as "treacherous" and came upon "two thievish coyotes, which I soon dispatched with my pistol."

But Adams had captured four bears, and he set upon the task of training them. "It is with bears as it is with children," Adams said. "If the right course be taken, their natural characters may be modified and improved to such a degree as to be a subject of wonder." He claimed to have "changed savage and ferocious natures to affection and gentleness."

His methods were not always gentle. With the black bear cubs, Adams helped acclimatize them to humans by having them sleep next to him. But the grizzlies were a year old, used to freedom, and harder to train. Lady Washington was especially resistant, and snapped at her trainer at every opportunity. Adams's solution was brutal but effective—what he called the "first lesson subjection."

Adams cut himself a stout cudgel and "began vigorously warming her jacket. This made her furious; it would, indeed, be difficult to describe her violence, the snarls she uttered, and the frothing anger she exhibited." Finally, he said, "She acknowledged herself well corrected, and lay down exhausted. It is, beyond question, a cruel spectacle to see a man thus taking an animal and whipping it into subjection; but when a bear has once grown up, untutored, as large as the Lady was, this is the only way to lay the foundation of an education." The male grizzly, Jackson, also proved more tractable after a bit of brutality.

Adams continued to collect specimens until he'd achieved quite a menagerie, which he carried to Portland and put aboard the good ship *Mary Ann*, bound for Boston and brother William. The animals arrived safely and were sold to museums and other exhibitors, serving "to spread a knowledge of the Pacific Coast of the United States," Adams said. He kept only Lady Washington, who he could not imagine being without. The next year he traveled with her through the Rockies and back over the mountains to California. "I felt for her an affection which I have seldom given to any human being," Adams said.

Soon after, Adams trained the Lady to carry his pack (usually full of the game he killed), and eventually she "bore my camp equipage and other heavy burdens with willingness, and even alacrity."

In 1854, back in central California near the headwaters of the Merced River, Adams acquired Ben Franklin, aka Gentle Ben, the grizzly he called "the flower of his race, my firmest friend, the boon companion of my after-years." He acquired him and a second cub as a week-old newborn, after dispatching his mother in front of their den. For sustenance, he convinced a mother greyhound to suckle them for several weeks before they were weaned and became accustomed to meat.

Although he did in all manner of animals with relish, including many black and grizzly bears (indeed, such killing constitutes the bulk of his autobiography), Adams was quite solicitous of his captives. He even made Ben a set of buckskin and elk leather booties when his feet got sore from walking on sharp rocks. Later, after capturing some bears that were sent via Stockton to customers in South America, Adams caught the mighty 1,500-pound grizzly Samson in a trap. He describes the bear as the largest of his species then taken alive.

Adams sold meat and hides from the animals he hunted to emigrants along the Oregon and Mormon Trails, and also traded at Fort Bridger—where he may have encountered Jim Bridger or Louis Vasquez.

Adams (whose primary activity was hunting animals, not training them) was no doubt sincere about loving his bears, even as he was killing their kindred. To Ben he even owed his life, since the ursine companion defended him during an attack by a "huge grizzly."

Adams recounts,

> That was one of the narrowest escapes I ever had in all my hunting; and, as my preservation was due to Ben, the circumstance explains, to some extent, the partiality I have felt towards that noble animal. He has borne the scars of the combat upon his front ever since; and I take pride in pointing them out to persons who, I think, can appreciate my feelings towards him.

It never seems to occur to Adams that his admiration for Ben should be transferred to the rest of his species, since he shoots every other bear—black and grizzly—he sees. But every hunter grows weary of the chase, and finally Adams makes his way to San Jose, then Santa Clara, and finally to San Francisco, showing his animals along the way and eventually establishing the Pacific Museum.

"I have by degrees gathered all my animals together, and have them now, a goodly company, about me," Adams said. "As I look around upon them I am reminded of the freshness and freedom of the forests, and live over again in imagination the golden days when I trod, in pleasure and in joy, upon the mountain side. Lady Washington, Ben Franklin—noble Ben, and his foster-brother Rambler [a greyhound]; they are all here."

"Lord" George Sanger's Royal Menagerie. It was the first circus to use three rings. (Wikipedia)

CIRCUS ANIMALS: A SHORT HISTORY

As early as 140 BC, Roman leaders realized that "bread and circuses" were the way to keep the people appeased. Chariot races, acrobatics, and trained animals were the fare—though hardly the acts we think of today. Zebras and ostriches pulled chariots, and all manner of exotic creatures fought gladiators, or were targeted for slaughter in staged hunts.

Inauguration games at the Roman Colosseum in 81 AD lasted one hundred days, and resulted in the deaths of more than nine thousand animals, including lions, horses, elephants, leopards, giraffes (led in through specially raised gates) hyenas, tigers—even hippos and rhinos. The games killed so many animals that some (the European wild horse, the great auk, the Eurasian lynx) became extinct.

Phillip Astley (1742–1814) is the father of the modern western circus, and his work with trained horses grew out of his experiences as a cavalryman in the 15th British Dragoons. He combined, for the first time, trick riding with performing animals and a clown in a single ring.

Horse-riding exhibits were going on in the US as early as 1724, and entrepreneurs displayed a lion (1716), a camel (1721), and polar bear (1733). The first real circus in the US was organized in Philadelphia by John Bill Ricketts in 1793, and was so popular that an enthralled George Washington donated Jack, the horse he'd ridden during the Revolutionary War.

Elephants entered the scene in 1805 when a Somers, New York, farmer named Hachaliah Bailey bought one, hoping to use it as a plow animal. But she ate too much, so he took her on the road as a traveling exhibit, charging up to fifty cents for the privilege of seeing such an exotic creature. The act made money, and soon other area farmers went into the traveling menagerie business. By 1835 they'd founded the Zoological Institute, and began to expand by adding human acts, leading to circuses as we know them today.

John "Grizzly" Adams captured live bears, wolves, and other animals to feed a growing demand for them as performers and exhibits. "Lord" George Sanger's circus, the first to use three rings, arrived in style during the late nineteenth century, led by a huge ten-ton carriage, carrying Nero, the circus lion (with a lamb at her feet). Camels, elephants, and other beasts followed behind. By 1903, there were almost one hundred circuses and menageries touring in the US, many by rail.

Were these performing animals treated humanely? Absolutely not. They had little or no legal protection in the US until the Animal Welfare Act was amended to include exhibition animals in 1970.

Adams found he had nothing to regret. "I have looked on death in many forms, and trust that I can meet it whenever it comes with a stout heart and steady nerves," he said. "If I could choose, I would wish, since it was my destiny to become a mountaineer and grizzly bear hunter of California, to finish my career in the Sierra Nevada. There would I fain lay down with the Lady, Ben, and Rambler at my side; there, surely, I could find rest through the long future, among the eternal rocks and evergreen pines."

But that's not what, in fact, happened. Poor Ben Franklin got sick and died of unknown causes in 1858, which considerably disheartened Adams. The passing was noted in San Francisco's *Evening Bulletin* under the headline, "Death of a Distinguished Native Californian."

Instead of resuming life as a hunter, Adams went in the opposite direction—he made arrangements with the great showman P. T. Barnum and took his remaining animals to New York, which in those days before the Panama Canal required a three-month trip around Cape Horn. He was at least partially motivated by a desire to once again see Cylena, from whom he'd been separated ten years, and provide for his family.

During the long voyage, the head injury Adams sustained from the same grizzly who also wounded Ben opened up and became infected, such that he was in no great state upon arriving in New York.

Adams was reunited with Cylena in New York, but she was soon relegated to serving as his nurse—the once-rugged mountain man's health was failing.

Despite this, a buckskin-clad Adams paraded his animals down Broadway, and the "Old Grizzy Adams" act was a huge hit with Barnum's crowds in New York. The troupe also traveled through Connecticut and Massachusetts under the showman's baton during the summer of 1860. His wound grew worse, and when he finally completed his contract and made his way to his family in Neponset, Massachusetts, near Boston, he took to his bed and never rose from it. Satisfied that he had lived life to the fullest, Adams—probably then just forty-eight—died with a smile on his face. Barnum paid for the funeral.

WHAT HE SAID

As P. T. Barnum told it, Adams on his deathbed was asked about his faith, and replied,

> I have attended preaching every day, Sundays and all, for the last six years. Sometimes an old grizzly gave me the sermon, sometimes it was a panther; often it was the thunder and lightning, the tempest or the hurricane, on the peaks of the Sierra Nevada or in the gorges of the Rocky Mountains. But whatever preached to me, it always taught me the majesty of the Creator and revealed to me the undying and unchanging love of our kind Father in Heaven. Although I am a pretty rough customer, I fancy my heart is in about the right place, and look with confidence for that rest which I so much need, and which I have never enjoyed upon earth.

Grizzly Adams on tour. The trained bears were a draw. (Wikipedia)

Henry Bergh: The real friend of animals.
(Wikipedia)

THE ANIMALS' REAL FRIEND: HENRY BERGH

A contemporary of John "Grizzly" Adams who is more worthy of praise for his humane treatment of animals is the much more urbane Henry Bergh, who founded the American Society for the Prevention of Cruelty to Animals (ASPCA) in New York in 1866. Born wealthy, he took on the animals' cause after seeing horses cruelly beaten during his service with the American Legation to Tsar Alexander II's Russia.

Bergh personally took on dog, rat, and cockfighting, operated the first ambulances for horses, and went after slaughterhouse abuses. He also wrote a "Declaration of the Rights of Animals," campaigning for what he called "these mute servants of mankind."

The ASPCA won the right to enforce anti-cruelty laws, and it went after abusers of horses, livestock, pigeons, cats, and dogs. Bergh, wearing a special badge, became known as "The Great Meddler," and astonished onlookers when—in top hat and spats—he admonished the driver of a coal cart for whipping his horse in 1866. It was groundbreaking when, in 1867, a man drew a two-year prison sentence for beating a cat to death.

When Bergh died in 1888, thirty-seven of what was then thirty-eight states used the ASPCA to fight animal abuse. Ironically, protecting children took longer. The New York Society for the Prevention of Cruelty to Children modeled itself on the ASPCA, and Bergh was one of its first vice presidents. It was launched in response to child-labor abuses, and after nine-year-old Mary Ellen McCormack was found tied to a bed and brutally beaten by her foster parents, in 1874.

PIERRE LOUIS AND BENITO VASQUEZ

THE SPANISH
TRADERS

BENITO VASQUEZ AND HIS SON, PIERRE LOUIS VASQUEZ

THE LEGEND

What's interesting in Louis Vasquez's story is that this important mountain man is little known today, but his partner, Jim Bridger, is virtually a household name. Louis's father, the Spaniard Benito Vasquez, has an equally interesting history, tied in as it is with the famous John Colter, but he's little remembered, either. Perhaps the American historical record wasn't ready for mountain men of Spanish and French ancestry.

HOW THEY GET IT WRONG

The sin is one of omission; there's precious little on either Vasquez, father or son, in the public record. Louis, despite building a significant fort that bore his name, and a second with the celebrated Jim Bridger as a way station for emigrants and traders—apparently didn't interest the dime novelists or newspaper scribes. But he prospered without the attention of the media or Wild West shows.

*Jim Bridger is well remembered today; his partner, Louis Vasquez,
less so. (Uintah County Regional History Center)*

WHAT WE ACTUALLY KNOW

Louis Vasquez was something rare—a second-generation mountain man. His father, Benito Vasquez, was from Galicia, Spain, and came over from there with the Spanish army in 1769 as it sought to take over French possessions.

Benito left army life in 1772 to take up the burgeoning fur trade, and in 1773 received a land grant from the Spanish lieutenant governor, at St. Louis. He married Marie-Julie Papin, a French-Canadian, in St. Louis in 1774. They had no less than twelve children, ten of whom lived to adulthood. Pierre-Luis (later Louis) Vasquez was the last of them, born in 1798.

There's not a whole lot on Benito Andres Vasquez, who lived until 1810. In 1794, in a meeting at St. Louis, what was then the Missouri fur business was divided up, and Benito was one of four to be given an equal share of the trade with the Kansas Indians. He was party to the formation of the Missouri Company ("La Compagnie de Commerce pour la Découverte des Nations du Haut-Missouri") that same year, with the purpose of exploring and trading in the Upper Missouri River area.

In 1794, Benito spent the winter with the Kansas Indians. The next year, on his way back to St. Louis, his group was waylaid by a band of 160 Iowas, who plundered their boats and carried off two of the party, beating them and leaving them at the mouth of the Kansas River, naked and without food or guns.

According to Le Roy Reuben Hafen, one of the few writers to explore this period in depth, the French were pioneers in exploration and colonization, founding both St. Louis and New Orleans and exploring the Mississippi River and its tributaries. Treaties in 1762 and 1763 ceded most of France's North American territory to Great Britain, and Louisiana to Spain. Many fur traders remained and prospered. Some worked for Hudson's Bay Company.

In 1807, an expedition led by veteran trader Manuel Lisa, who established the Big Horn River Company, set out with two keelboats and fifty to sixty men toward the Three Forks region, where they intended to build a post for trading with the Indians. Second in command was Benito Vasquez.

En route, a man named Antoine Bissonette deserted, and Lisa aide George Druillard (a Corps of Discovery veteran) tracked him down and shot him. He died on the boat back to St. Charles, and Druillard was later tried for murder (he was acquitted). The party had an unsettling encounter with the Arikaras, but escaped without bloodshed. On their journey upriver, they met the guide John Colter (also a former member of the Corps of Discovery), who agreed to help them get to the Big Horn. Colter convinced them this was a better place than Three Forks, because of friendly Crows nearby.

Lisa and Vasquez built their log trading post, Fort Manuel (other locations also had this name), at the mouth of the Big Horn, and an 1890 account from Hubert Howe Bancroft says they were "probably the first to erect a fort in this part of the Rocky Mountains," trading in "peltries" that were equally from Montana and Wyoming. Colter was asked to alert the local tribes that the fort was open and trading.

In 1808, Colter hooked up at Three Forks with John Potts, who signed a $424 note for trading supplies to Manuel Lisa. While trapping, they had an encounter with the Blackfeet, and Potts (who'd shot at the Indians) was killed. But Colter—who'd been stripped naked—was given a chance to run for his life. Colter's Run, it's called, and a big reason we remember his name today.

According to Bancroft, "[Colter] was pursued by several hundred Indians, the ground that he had to pass over being covered with prickly pear, which lacerated his naked feet. Such exertion did he make that the blood gushed from his mouth and nostrils."

The Perilous West by Larry E. Morris relates that Colter hid in a beaver dam. He then spent nine days in a trek to the friendly Mandans, "without even mowkasons" to

Louis Vasquez, a second-generation mountain man who took up the fur trade in 1772. (Used by permission, Utah State Historical Society)

protect his feet, "subsisting on such berries as providence threw in his way." He arrived famished, blistered, and with horribly swollen legs. Vasquez was one of the first to hear the amazing story.

In 1809, Vasquez, Colter (who was the first white man to visit what became Jackson Hole and Yellowstone Park), and others closed the fort and, with fifteen beaver skins and ten buffalo robes, went to trade at the Mandan villages on the Missouri. In 1810, Colter led a party back to Fort Manuel and reopened it, but a group of the trappers were attacked by the Blackfeet, two were killed, and all the skins were lost.

Colter vowed not to visit the area again, and Fort Manuel was closed permanently in 1813. Colter then assisted William Clark, who'd become governor of the Missouri Territory that year, with mapping the Northwest for the 1814 edition of his journals. He had vital details of the Yellowstone and Wind River area.

Given all this, you'd think the last thing Louis Vasquez would do was pursue the family business, but in fact he did. Louis was twelve when his father died, but he evidently had fur trading in his blood. In 1823, he joined a fur-trading company led by General William Ashley (of the ill-fated Hugh Glass expedition). Vasquez obtained the first license to trade with the Pawnee that same year.

In 1832, Louis Vasquez served as clerk to Robert Campbell, and helped send a supply train to the Mountain Man Rendezvous (that

Above: John Colter's historical marker in Stuarts Draft, Virginia. (Wikipedia)

Right: Jim Bridger sculpture by David Alan Clark at Fort Bridger, Montana. (Wikipedia)

year held at Pierre's Hole). The next winter, he was trading with the Crows for furs, bringing eighty packs of buffalo robes to Fort William.

In 1835, Louis Vasquez and Andrew Sublette, having obtained a trading license from William Clark, by then the Superintendent of Indian Affairs, built the adobe Fort Vasquez (since rebuilt, now a museum) on the South Platte River, near the Trappers' Trail in what we now know as Platteville, Colorado. According to the museum's history, "[Vasquez and Sublette] wanted to be near the Cheyenne and Arapaho Indians, who traded buffalo robes for blankets, beads, kettles, knives, guns, ammunition and other manufactured goods."

"Each year," the history continues,

> the traders traveled to St. Louis with their furs and returned with
> wagonloads of trade goods drawn by mule teams along the Santa Fe
> Trail and then north to the fort. Vasquez and Sublette employed as
> many as 22 men each year to serve as traders or hunters for the fort. The
> founders abandoned the fort in 1842 and its walls eroded into the soil."
> Unfortunately, there were four trading posts along the Upper South Platte
> River by 1837, so competition (especially for buffalo robes) was stiff.

Actually, the partners sold the fort in 1840, but Lock and Randolph, who bought it, went bankrupt, so Vasquez and Sublette couldn't collect. There's evidence that Vasquez was held in high regard by his men, because he went missing for a time, until Sublette's party found a letter from him sticking to a twig in the vicinity of Devil's Gate. According to William Anderson, a member of the party, "There was a shout of joy from the whole company. [The letter] was from Lew Vasquez, a great favorite of the mountaineers who had almost been given up for lost. This letter was his resurrection. . . . One old trapper said, 'Thank God he lives, and I shall hear his merry laugh again.'"

Poor Vasquez then hooked up with the legendary mountain man Jim Bridger (the very man Glass spared), and built Fort Bridger on Blacks Fork of the Green River. This

A period room at Fort Bridger. (Carol Highsmith/Library of Congress)

was successful, and Fort Bridger became a popular place to stop on the Oregon Trail. Vasquez was the likely manager, because Bridger was often out trapping.

According to the Wyoming State Historical Society, "Their first 'fort' consisted of two rude double-log houses about 40 feet in length, joined with a pen for horses. They also boasted a blacksmith's shop, something that many emigrants welcomed after months on the trails." But it wasn't fancy. Emigrant Edwin Bryant reported, "The buildings are two or three miserable cabins, rudely constructed and bearing but a faint resemblance to habitable houses."

THE FRONTIER'S SPANISH ACCENT

Though you'd never know it by watching traditional westerns, a knowledge of Spanish or French was very useful for fur traders and mountain men. Louis Vasquez was far from the only Hispanic fur trader on the frontier. Here are two colorful figures.

Manuel Alvarez was born in Albegas, Spain, in 1794, but was in Mexico by 1818. From there, he journeyed to New York, then to Missouri, and finally to Santa Fe, New Mexico, by 1824. He was a successful trader there for several years then became a fur trapper from 1831 to 1833, first as a free agent then as an agent for the American Fur Company.

Alvarez was highly respected in the fur business, and in 1833 was placed in charge of forty men trapping on Henry's Fork and the Yellowstone. That same year, he received a note "for services rendered" in the fur trade for $1,325.98, a huge sum at the time.

By 1834, Alvarez was back in Santa Fe as a general trader. After the US acquired New Mexico in 1848, the educated and erudite Alvarez (who spoke English, French, and Spanish) became interested in politics. Although not a citizen, Alvarez was American consul to Mexico from 1839 to 1846. He was also a leader in pushing for the New Mexico Territory to become a state (which it did in 1912, long after Alvarez's death in 1856).

Marcelino Baca, of Mexican heritage, was born in Taos, New Mexico, around 1808. According to the 1859 *Life in the Far West*, he was acclaimed as "the best trapper and hunter in the mountains and ever first in the fight."

Baca (who also worked as a gold miner) began accompanying American trapping companies in the 1820s, when it was difficult for non-Mexican trappers to get a foothold in the territory. He began trapping on his own in 1832 or 1833, and by 1835 was a member of Jim Bridger's American Fur Company (remaining through the winter of 1837 to 1838).

That winter, Baca was shot in the foot by Blackfeet during an encounter on the Yellowstone River. He escaped further injury by leaping down a fifty-foot bluff. At the end of 1838, the Pawnee captured Baca and were preparing to torture him to death when the chief's daughter (shades of Pocahontas) intervened to spare his life. Baca was true to his new love, married her, and had three children by her. The children were later baptized into the Catholic Church in Taos.

Baca later became a farmer and rancher, and traded with local Indians—some of whom were friendly, and some of whom nearly killed him and did kill his brother. When the Civil War broke out, Baca joined the New Mexico Volunteers and was killed in a battle with the Texans on February 21, 1862.

Among the travelers to California who enjoyed the rude accommodations at Fort Bridger in 1846 was the ill-fated Donner Party. They'd decided to take a dangerous "shortcut," the Hastings Cutoff, which both Bridger and Vasquez advocated (because it drove wagon traffic past their fort).

James Fraser Reed, a leader of the Donner Party, had earlier praised Bridger and Vasquez as "excellent and accommodating gentlemen," but after he learned the truth about their reasons for advocating the Hasting Cutoff, he made a rather serious charge against them in the *Pacific Rural Press* in 1871. He wrote that friends of his had "left letters with Mr. Vasquez—Mr. Bridger's partner—directing me to take the [regular] route by way of Fort Hall, and by no means to go the Hastings Cut-off. Vasquez, being interested in having the new route traveled (otherwise the emigration would use the Greenwood Cut-off and miss Fort Bridger) kept these letters" [in his pocket, says one account]. The Donner group left the fort for a nightmare journey into cannibalism that still resonates today.

The men who ran Fort Bridger were generally believed to be honest, but an 1843 letter from William Laidlaw, who ran Fort Union, cast doubt on the characters of both. Bridger, it said, "is not a man calculated to manage men, and in my opinion will never succeed in making profitable returns." Partner Vasquez, it added, is "if possible, more unable than he, as by drinking and frolicking at the Platte, he neglected his business."

Good businessman or not, Vasquez returned to St. Louis in 1846, married a Kentucky-born widow named Narcissa Land Ashcraft, and took on her two children. The new family, after briefly returning to Fort Bridger in 1847, opened a store in Salt Lake City, and also operated a flat-bottomed toll boat that was used to ferry wagons across the Green River.

Vasquez and Bridger sold Fort Bridger to the Mormon Church in 1855, by which time Bridger was the active partner. Events were dramatic. The Mormon Pioneer Company had arrived at Fort Bridger in 1847, but found the prices unnecessarily high. So were the tensions. A group of Mormon settlers claimed that Bridger was selling ammunition and liquor to the Indians, violating federal law.

Brigham Young, the Society reports, sent in the Mormon militia in 1853, causing Bridger to flee. The Mormons controlled the fort until 1855, when Bridger came back, after complaining to US senator (and general) B. F. Butler that one hundred thousand dollars in goods had been stolen from him. After several months of negotiations he and Vasquez sold out their interests.

Fort Bridger became a military outpost in 1858. Now it is a major attraction and state park. Vasquez eventually moved back to Missouri, and died there in Westport in 1868, by which time he had seven of his own children, in addition to the two stepchildren.

Vaqueros in California around 1830. They set the template for the cowboy. (Wikipedia)

VAQUEROS: THE MEXICAN COWBOYS

The word "vaquero" means herder, based on the Spanish word "vaca," for cow. According to *American Cowboy* magazine, as soon as the Spanish arrived in Mexico in 1519 they built ranches stocked with imported horses and cattle from Spain, and by the early 1700s that way of life had spread to what is now Texas, New Mexico, and Arizona.

National Geographic reports that even as early as 1600, some twenty years before the Pilgrims landed on Plymouth Rock, "adventurous *criollos* (Spanish-born Americans) and *mestizos* (mixed Spanish and Indian settlers) pushed past the Rio Grande River to take advantage of land grants in the kingdom of New Mexico, which included most of the western states."

Much of what we think of as cowboy culture derives from these Mexican vaqueros, including branding, specialized saddles, roping, and the use of a lariat (called "reatas").

After the Franciscan missions were built in what is now California, beginning in 1769, that territory had a foothold in the livestock industry, too. Since there wasn't much of a local market, the meat had to be transported back to Mexico, and so roundups and cattle herding along established trails became ritualized.

Soon these Mexican cowboys were everywhere, cutting romantic figures. "Known for expert horsemanship and roping skills, vaqueros were said to only dismount for a chance to dance with pretty girls," *American Cowboy* said. After the Mexican-American War of 1846 to 1848, and the Gold Rush that followed soon after, the demand for meat grew, and more and more Anglo cowboys were on the scene. They developed their own version of *vaquero* culture. The word "buckaroo" is derived from "vaquero."

There were millions of lost, strayed, and wild longhorn cattle in the Texan brush. The Anglo settlers who began settling there in 1821 rounded them up, and soon a big and region-defining industry was born—one that should fondly remember its Hispanic roots.

WHAT THEY SAID

Both Benito and Louis Vasquez wrote letters that survive. In 1798, Benito Vasquez wrote a flowery letter [in Spanish] to Gayoso de Lemos then the Spanish governor-general of New Spain. His tone is anguished, but carefully respectful. He'd been granted the exclusive right to the fur trade "in the Kansas nation in the Missouri," but the promised formal decree of the concession hadn't arrived. Benito couldn't sell his merchandise or settle his debts. "I find myself at the end of my resources," Benito wrote, "and have never seen myself in such a straitened condition." Unless the decree was forthcoming, he said, "I see no other alternative [than] to deliver myself over to great poverty."

Under the influence of wine, Benito had insulted the previous governor-general, Francisco Luis Hector, baron of Carondelet, accusing him of acting like a "rogue," "thief," and "usurper." For this crime he was under arrest for thirty-five days.

Louis wrote his brother, Benito Jr., in 1834 [in French]: "I am not coming down [to Missouri] this year . . . I beg you to write to me and give me the detail news from all. . . . If you could procure for me a few novels, Mr. Campbell would be pleased to bring them to me. . . . Embrace the whole family for me. Tell them I love them all." So he was a literate man, with time to read.

KIT CARSON

FAMOUS FOR ALL THE

WRONG REASONS

KIT CARSON

THE LEGEND

There's no doubt that Kit Carson was the quintessential, larger-than-life mountain man. In the public imagination, Carson is forever either blazing a trail through the wilderness for grateful trappers and explorers, or fighting Indians—always with cause.

HOW THEY GET IT WRONG

Carson's actual achievements were considerable, but he was far from perfect. And because this somewhat taciturn figure was an ideal subject for nineteenth century pulp fiction, his real life became entwined with a mountain of myth.

Carson's legend was built while he was still alive and vigorous, which meant he often failed to live up to his admirers' expectations. For one thing, he was short, just five feet four inches tall, but is described as "of perfect proportions and Herculean stature" in *Kit Carson: Prince of the Gold Hunters* ("founded on actual facts") by pulp fiction hack Charles Averill. The same book credits Carson with discovering gold in California.

Carson actually wrote—dictated would be more accurate—an autobiography in 1856, but it was dry as dust (not even mentioning the two Indian wives) and only one hundred pages. Carson's literary agent offered the rewrite to Washington Irving, who said no, and then to army surgeon DeWitt Clinton Peters, a friend of Carson's. And Peters went to town writing a much-embellished tome entitled *The Life and Adventures of Kit Carson . . . from Facts Narrated by Himself.*

As Jill Lepore relates in *The New Yorker,* Carson wrote that the saddlery business "did not suit me." Peters, who added four hundred pages, recounts it thus: "Saddlery is an honorable employment; but saddlery never made a greater mistake than when it strove to hitch to its traces the bold impulse, the wild yearning, the sinewy muscle of Kit Carson."

It's striking how Peters, in his preface, takes pains to assert the veracity of his tale. He claims, "The pages here presented to the public form a book of facts. . . . The savage

Kit Carson was a strange mix of impulses.
(Brady-Handy photographic collection/
Library of Congress)

warrior and hunter is presented, stripped of all the decorations with which writers of fiction have dressed him."

Carson was, at first, amused. Peters had "laid it on a leetle too thick," Carson said. Oddly enough, though, when Carson was dying he lay quietly, smoking his pipe, while his doctor read him passages from that book. Who doesn't want to think of himself as a hero?

But worse fabulists than Peters were to come. In the forty years after 1860, an almost unrecognizable Kit Carson appeared in more than seventy dime novels, none of which paid him any royalties.

Carson was "dismayed at the scope of his growing fame," as noted on History.net. When he first encountered *Prince of the Gold Hunters*, Carson said the book was "the first of its kind I had ever seen, in which I was made a great hero, slaying Indians by the hundreds."

At the time, Carson was pursuing Ann White, who'd been captured by the Jicarilla Apaches. But she was found in their recently abandoned camp, horribly abused and recently killed by an arrow through her heart—along with a copy of Averill's book, which included an account in which Carson bravely rescued just such a woman. At first he was amused, then appalled. "Knowing that I lived near, I have often thought that [had] Mrs. White read the book, she prayed for my appearance, and that she might be saved," Carson said.

The Imagined West writes about this encounter: "The fictional Carson became the standard for the real Carson, and the connection between the two goes beyond this, for the story of the incident comes to us in a book, written by the actual Carson, to capitalize on the market the mythic Carson had created for him," it said.

In *Blood and Thunder*, Hampton Sides adds, "This was the first time that the real Kit Carson had come in contact with his own myth." Much later, when Carson was offered a copy of Averill's book by a friend, he threatened to "burn the damn thing."

Dime novels know no bounds. In *Rocky Mountain Kit's Last Scalp Hunt*, he is said to have "ridden into Sioux camps unattended and alone, [then] ridden out again, but with the scalps of their greatest warriors at his belt." In *The Fighting Trapper: Kit Carson to the*

Rescue, he is shown with fierce countenance, killing a different Indian with each hand. Another goes one better—he's killing Indians with *one* hand, while holding a beautiful rescued maiden in the other. *True West* recounts, "When it was shown to him he glanced at it and modestly replied, 'That thar may be true, but I hain't got no recollection of it.'"

The legend found new mediums. An idealized Carson was the Indian-fighting subject of a 1940 film, and a fanciful TV show (which ran from 1951 to 1955) called *The Adventures of Kit Carson*—complete with Mexican sidekick.

Carson was probably surprised to hear of "friends" he never actually met. One dubious fellow named "Captain William F. Drannan" claimed to have been Carson's boon companion for many years, and delivered the fictional *Thirty-One Years on the Plains and in the Mountains* in 1899. But there's not much evidence that the actual Drannan—believed to be in the hotel business around Seattle and Portland at the time he wrote the book—was present for many of the events described, or had such a central role.

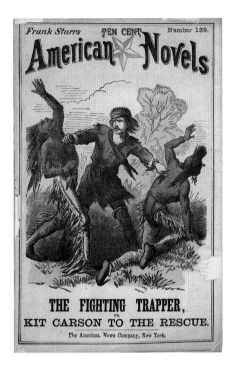

An 1874 dime novel starring an idealized Kit Carson. He didn't recognize himself. (Wikipedia)

Some sources say Drannan's wife actually wrote *Thirty-One Years*, and a volume called *Frontier Legend* by Walter Bate throws all kinds of dirt on Drannan (who also wrote another questionable tome called *Chief of Scouts*). Bate calls him Carson's "pseudo frontier comrade." Drannan doesn't make it into Carson biographies, he wasn't chief of scouts, nor was he a Texas Ranger (which is claimed on his tombstone). But further burnishing of the Carson legend is on every page of Drannan's book.

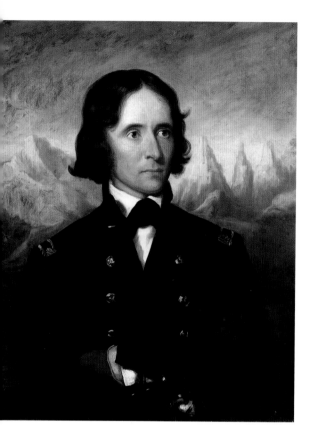

John C. Frémont as painted by George Healy. (Wikipedia)

A LIFE REMEMBERED

I entered "Kit Carson" into eBay and came up with the following: a "Little Golden Book" about the famous scout (from the "High Lights of History" series); signed sterling silver Kit Carson earrings in the shape of hot peppers; *The Golden Stamp Book of Kit Carson*; *Kit Carson: Mountain Man*, the 1961 Scholastic biography by Margaret Bell; *Kit Carson's Life and Adventures* by Dewitt Peters from 1874; *Dear Old Kit* by Harvey Lewis Carter (1968); *A Ride With Kit Carson: Across The Great American Desert and Through the Rocky Mountains* by George D. Brewerton (1969 first edition); *Kit Carson's Autobiography* (1935); *Kit Carson: Folk Hero and Man* by Noel Gerson (1964); *Kit Carson and the Indians* by Thomas Dunlay (2005); *A Newer World: Kit Carson, John C. Frémont and the Claiming of the American West* by David Roberts (2001); and at least a dozen other biographies.

I could buy a sterling silver pendant of a cowboy on a horse with lasso "designed by Kit Carson"; an 1848 copy of the *National Intelligencer* newspaper with the headline "Frontier Scout Kit Carson to Join Frémont Expedition to the West"; a sterling silver Kit Carson sheriff badge ("rare"); and a whole lot of other stuff. If greatness was measured by the ephemera we leave behind, Kit Carson would tower nearly as high as Davy Crockett and Daniel Boone.

WHAT WE ACTUALLY KNOW

It's hard to know the real Kit Carson. The 1888 *Story of the Wild West*, accurately asserts:

> No character of which history gives any account presents more anomalous peculiarities than that of Kit Carson. His whole nature was enigmatic, for no two persons, however intimate they may have been with him, whether on the plains or in the councils of white men or Indians, could agree in their estimation of his traits of character.

Kit Carson in a beaver hat. (Wikipedia)

The historic Carson was born in Kentucky in 1809, but after that the legend and the facts diverge. He became an apprentice saddle maker, and hated it. By the time he was eighteen, he was traveling with trappers in New Mexico (initially as the cook), and gradually became an experienced guide in the West. He learned to speak Spanish (better than he spoke English), fought Indians (especially Apaches, but also Crows and Cheyenne), and was shot not once but twice. He was married three times, twice to Indians. And he was illiterate.

Carson hooked up with the noted explorer of the Rockies John C. Frémont (after meeting him on a steamboat in 1842), and helped blaze new trails through Wyoming, Utah, Colorado, and California on three expeditions that concluded in 1845. Frémont (known as "The Pathfinder") wrote a book about his first expedition that turned him into a compass-wielding celebrity, probably the most famous explorer of his day.

According to David Roberts's *A Newer World*, Frémont's writing, including government reports, which were popular reading at the time, also promoted Carson as a hero, helping turn him into "the country's most famous mountain man, scout and Indian fighter."

The time with Carson was a high point for Frémont: Later, he became a US senator from California, but served only briefly, and lost as the Republican Party's nominee for president in 1856. He was later cashiered by Abraham Lincoln after a short stint running the Union Army's Western Department. After being convicted in a swindle, he died in poverty.

Carson often spoke admiringly of Indians he'd encountered. He reportedly spoke seven of their languages, and understood their ways better than most. He was an effective Indian agent for the Ute tribe. But his reputation for fairness is tarnished. In fact, he was heavily involved in notable atrocities, including the 1845 massacre of 175 northern California Indians who were, on dubious grounds, believed to be on the verge of attacking a white settlement.

In 1846, at Klamath Lake in southern Oregon during Frémont's third expedition, three of his men were killed in an Indian attack, probably by the Modocs. "The Indians had commenced the war with us without cause," Carson later said. "I thought they should be chastised in a summary manner."

A few days later, led by Carson, a force of eleven men attacked a Klamath fishing village, and according to Hampton Sides's *Blood and Thunder*, "fired away with impunity." In a few minutes, twenty-one Indians lay dead, after which their village was put to the torch. "We gave them something to remember," Carson said. "They were severely punished." Some accounts say many women and children were among the dead, since many of the men were out hunting. The Klamath are culturally related to the Modocs, but were then bitter enemies.

And from 1863 to 1864, Carson, under the US military command of General James Henry Carleton, supervised ruinous campaigns against the Mescalero Apaches and the Navajos in New Mexico. He was particularly brutal to the latter, destroying their fruit trees and crops (nearly two million pounds of food), taking or killing their horses and livestock, breaking their pots and baskets, and then—after the starving Indians surrendered—moving more than nine thousand of them on the three-hundred-mile "Long Walk" to Fort Sumner in the Bosque Redondo region in the eastern part of the state. At least two hundred Navajo died along the way, and when they were finally released in 1868, three thousand had died at Bosque Redondo.

The gradual disappearance of the Navajos was, to Carleton, part of God's plan. "God wills that one race of men—as in the races of lower animals—shall disappear off the

face of the earth and give place to another race," he said. "The Red Man of America is passing away!" For his work, Carleton received a commendation from President Abraham Lincoln.

It wasn't only Indians. During the Frémont California expedition in 1846, Carson also carried out the cold-blooded murder of three Mexicans, including a pair of twins, who were no more than merely suspected of involvement in an earlier crime. It wasn't racism— Carson was Catholic, married to a Hispanic woman, and fluent in Spanish. But he was under orders from Frémont, and orders were important to him. When Frémont heard the three were dead, he said, "It is well."

Hampton Sides, who wrote *Blood and Thunder* about Carson's tragic role in the campaign against the Navajo, told the *Denver Post*,

> I started with the belief that Carson was a genocidal maniac. At the end of the book, my view of him was much more nuanced and multidimensional. I came to view him like a Mafia character, someone who would be interesting to meet, a colorful personality, but a man with a code that I didn't fully understand.

Kit Carson's former home in Taos, New Mexico. (Library of Congress)

WHAT HE SAID

Carson appears to have been, at least initially, proud of his work in subjugating the Navajo and Mescalero Apaches, claiming that any treaties made with them would be "as promises written in sand" because they had no real leaders. In 1864 he wrote an encomium to the role of his commander, James Henry Carleton.

This is the same Carleton who said of those Apaches,

> All Indian men of that tribe are to be killed whenever and wherever you can find them. . . . If the Indians send in a flag of truce say to the bearer . . . that you have been sent to punish them for their treachery and their crimes. That you have no power to make peace, that you are there to kill them wherever you can find them.

About the Navajo, he said, "Severity would be the most humane course."

Here's Carson on the same officer. "General J. H. Carleton was appointed to the command of this Department," it said,

> and with the greatest promptitude he turned his attention to the freeing of the Territory from these lawless savages. To this great work he brought many years' experience and a perfect knowledge of the means to effect that end. . . . He adopted a new policy, i.e., placing them on a reservation (the wisdom of which is already manifest); a new era dawned on New Mexico, and the dying hope of the people was again revived; never more I trust, to meet with disappointment. He first organized a force against the Mescalero Apaches, which I had the honor to command. After a short and inexpensive campaign, the Mescaleros were placed on their present reservation.

Of course, Carson was illiterate, so this would have had to be dictated, and it's hard to imagine him saying it.

Buffalo Bill was devastated at the early death of his son, Kit Carson Cody. (Wikipedia)

KIT CARSON AND BUFFALO BILL

Buffalo Bill thought enough of the famous scout to name his son Kit Carson Cody. Cody's sister, Helen Cody Wetmore, writes in her biography of her brother, "The first boy of the family was the object of the undivided interest of the outpost for a time, and names by the dozen were suggested. Major North offered 'Kit Carson' as an appropriate name for the son of a great scout and buffalo-hunter, and this was finally settled on."

Born in 1870, the boy, who wore long golden curls, appeared occasionally in dad's Wild West show. But young Kit lived only six years, catching scarlet fever in 1876. He died in his father's arms. "He was too good for this world," Cody said.

Did the two frontiersmen ever meet? You bet. In Cody's autobiography, he relates, "While I was hunting for the Kansas Pacific Railway, I had the pleasure, in the fall of 1867, of meeting the celebrated Kit Carson, one of, if not the oldest and most noted scout, guide and hunter that our western country has ever produced."

Carson, clearly ailing, was on his way to Washington, escorting Ute Chiefs for a meeting with the president. The two scouts also met upon Carson's return, but the trip was stressful. After Cody entertained him for a few days at Hays, Kansas, Carson left for Colorado, whereupon his wife died giving birth to their eighth child. Carson was devastated, and himself died soon after, at his son-in-law's home on Picket Wire Creek. His last words were, "Adios, compadres."

Wouldn't it have been great to know what these two old campaigners talked about?

It's possible that Carson had a change of heart later in life, and a diary of dubious provenance records him telling General William Sherman, "General, I'm not so sure the Great Spirit meant for us to take over Indian lands. Let me lead them back while they still have the will to live." But Hampton Sides's *Blood and Thunder* reports, "The possibility that Carson had undergone a complete reversal is tantalizing, but the provenance of this quote seems fishy. Certainly, it doesn't sound much like Carson."

The popular Kit, of course, comes down as definitely an Indian fighter, but a fairly benevolent one with a sense of humor and a gift for the vernacular. Edwin Sabin's 1914 *Kit Carson Days*, hardly a definitive source, relates this folksy tale, supposedly in Carson's voice:

> Well, I'll tell ye. I war down on the plains, an' the Comanches got after me. Thar war 'bout five hundred of 'em, an' they chased me. We run an' we run, an my hoss war killed an I [come to] a sort o' butte. Thar war a leetle split or cañon in it, an' I run up this. One big red rascal kep' right on my heels; my gun war busted, but I had my knife. The split narrered an' narrered, an got smaller an' smaller, an' suddenly it pinched out; an' thar I war, at the end. So I turned, with my knife, an' when he come on I struck at him. But the walls o' the split war so near together that I hit the rock, an' busted my knife squar' off at the hilt. When he seed that he give a big yell, for my scalp, an' at me he jumped. . . .

At this point, Carson paused for effect, and waited to be asked what happened next. "Then the Injun killed me," he roared.

Somehow we can imagine Carson drawling this tale. But after relating it, Sabin's book notes, "Considering that this episode is also attributed to Jim Bridger, as a favorite in his wide repertoire, we may accept the new version of it as 'trapper's talk.'" But the language, author Sabin said, "is like Kit Carson."

More succinctly, the same book recounts that an army officer met Carson and exclaimed, "So this is the great Kit Carson, who has made so many Indians run!" Carson replied, "Sometimes I run after *them* but most times they war runnin' after *me*."

BUFFALO BILL

THEATRICAL LIFE

MIXED FACT AND FICTION

WILLIAM "BUFFALO BILL" CODY

Buffalo Bill Cody in his prime. (Wikipedia)

THE LEGEND

Cody rode with the Pony Express circa 1860 when he was just fourteen years old, along the Oregon/California/Mormon Trail. It was a glamorous life, with fresh horse changes every twelve miles and life lived on the gallop. He became a Civil War soldier, an Indian fighter, and a dedicated buffalo hunter (from which his name is derived). In the Wild West after the war, he was acquainted with both "Wild Bill" Hickok and George Armstrong Custer, personally avenging the latter's death by killing a Cheyenne warrior and proclaiming, "The first scalp for Custer!"

Cody successfully turned his real-life adventures into the dramatic Wild West stage show, and used actual figures from his glory days—including both Wild Bill and Sitting Bull—to make the plays not only more realistic, but also not for the faint of heart. Sometimes Cody must have been confused about whether he was *being* a scout or merely *playing* one. According to Richard Slotkin's *Gunfighter Nation*, "Between 1872 and 1876 Cody alternated between his career as scout for the US Cavalry and his business as star of a series of melodramas in the East."

Louis S. Warren writes in *Buffalo Bill's America*, "Cody's childhood Mormon-and-Indian fighting, prospecting, Pony Express-riding, Hickok-knowing, bullwhacking saga was the foundation of his mythic western persona." And what a persona it was!

Buffalo Bill with Sitting Bull, who appeared regularly in his Wild West shows. (Library of Congress)

From left, Wild Bill Hickok, Texas Jack Omohundro, and Buffalo Bill. (Wikipedia)

HOW THEY GET IT WRONG

Cody was an authentic scout, soldier, and Indian fighter, but by the time he began starring in lurid and fanciful plays of his own invention, truth and fiction became hopelessly blurred.

Add in the fact that the dime novelist Ned Buntline (real name Edward Zane Carroll Judson Sr.), then the highest-paid writer in America, happened upon Cody's story after the 1869 Battle of Summit Springs against the Cheyenne Dog Soldiers. With little regard for actual events, he turned a bare-bones account into the bestselling *Buffalo Bill: The King of the Border Men*. From then on, Cody (who claimed to have personally killed the Cheyenne leader Tall Bull out of the saddle at thirty yards) was more celebrity than scout.

Reports PBS, "Buntline created a Buffalo Bill who ranked with Davy Crockett, Daniel Boone and Kit Carson in the popular imagination, and who was, like them, a mixture of incredible fact and romantic fiction." In 1872, Buntline introduced Cody to greasepaint by convincing him to perform in the novelist's play *Scouts of the Plains*, and he was a hit. The stage was set for a lucrative career, even if veracity suffered.

Hickok had preceded Cody in fame, as the subject of a much-read article in *Harper's Weekly*. That's one reason Buffalo Bill was so eager to place the two of them together at various historical junctures. Cody's autobiography is full of testimonials to Wild Bill's character. Both Bills ended up in dime novels that used their names but had little other basis in reality. About this time, Cody and Hickok started appearing together in plays, often of their own composition, around the West.

As noted, Hickok did not distinguish himself on stage. But according to Tom Rea of the Wyoming State Historical Society, "The plays were full of scrapes, escapes, daring rides, fights, rescues, noble heroes and evil villains—the same kind of stuff that thrilled the dime-novel readers."

When the Fifth Cavalry needed him for a war with the Plains Indians in the spring of 1875, Cody announced from the sage in Wilmington, Delaware, that he was giving up "play acting" for "the real thing." The army acquired a guide, but also an actor. Cody's scouting expeditions with the Fifth Cavalry in 1876 were undertaken in a bright red fireman's shirt and black velvet pants trimmed in scarlet, adorned with silver bells and elaborate embroidery. "This outfit was apparently some Eastern stage manager's idea of what Mexican vaqueros wore, and it was adopted for Cody's theatrical performances," reports History.net.

Despite protests that this wasn't how real scouts roamed the plains, Cody reportedly stuck with his colorful outfit throughout his time with the Fifth, bells and all. Cody was the most famous scout in America by this time, and he wanted to fully inhabit the part.

Cody did actually kill a Cheyenne during a skirmish with the Fifth in 1876, the only casualty that day, but the dead man was not as the showman claimed (and his supporters in the eastern press reported) the important chief, Yellow Hand. The deceased at Warbonnet Creek was actually Yellow Hair, the son of a chief but of no great significance himself. And maybe Cody did proclaim, "The first scalp for Custer!" but no one there that day recalls it. Some sources say Cody merely scored the dead Indian's hair after he'd been killed by others.

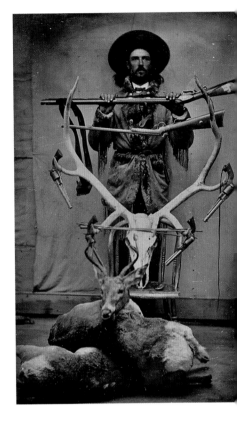

Early Buffalo Bill, quick with a gun and terror of the plain's animals. (Wikipedia)

Later, Cody sent the dead Indian's war bonnet and reeking scalp to his wife, Louisa, who fainted dead away when she opened the package. The treasures are now at the Buffalo Bill Museum in Cody, Wyoming.

Cody's fame really took off when he organized *Buffalo Bill's Wild West* shows in 1883, because the stage came alive with live buffaloes, Pony Express rides (featuring a horse change at full gallop), and a reenactment of Custer's Last Stand, featuring some Lakota who'd actually been there (including, for one season, Chief Sitting Bull himself). "Buffalo Bill's First Scalp for Custer" became one of the Wild West's popular melodramas. "King of the Cowboys" Buck Taylor took part, as did the legendary sharpshooter Annie Oakley.

One or another version of the *Wild West* shows toured for thirty years, even reaching Europe. In flush periods, the company numbered as high as 650, including trick riders and ropers, cowboys, Indians, stagehands, and animal trainers. Mark Twain was a fan. "Down to the smallest details, the show is genuine," he wrote in a letter to Cody. More accurate is novelist Larry McMurtry's assessment that Cody "created an illusion that successfully stood for a reality that had been almost wholly different."

Life and art continued to intermingle. In 1890, the army called Cody up one last time to help quell some late-period Indian uprising, and he brought some "friendly" Indians from his troupe along with him to help forge the peace. It actually worked.

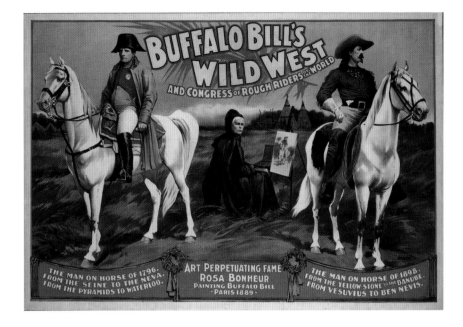

Opposite: Buffalo Bill poses with members of his Wild West troupe. (Wikipedia)

Buffalo Bill and Napoleon, too. (Library of Congress)

WHAT WE ACTUALLY KNOW

Cody, born in 1846, was most likely at school in Leavenworth, Kansas, when the Pony Express was extant. The scout claimed to have first been on duty in 1859, but the mail-carrying Pony Express wasn't launched until 1860. A second claimed stint, from 1860 to 1861, with Wild Bill part of the picture, is equally fanciful. He claimed to have traveled eighty-five miles between Three Crossings and Rocky Ridge, but in fact they're only twenty-five miles apart. Cody was only fourteen in 1860, so his claim to have ridden an epic 322 miles, virtually nonstop, to carry the mail seems dubious at best.

"William F. Cody never rode for the Pony Express at all," reports the Wyoming State Historical Society's Tom Rea. As a boy, Cody did drive some wagons and carry messages for Russell & Majors, the company that later started the Pony Express (at a princely twenty-five dollars a month), but his service wasn't all that glamorous.

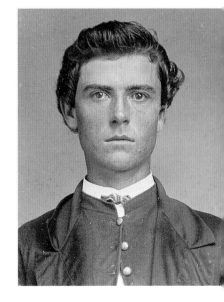

Buffalo Bill at 19. Pony Express rider? Probably not. (Wikipedia)

Above: Frank E. Webner, a for-real Pony Express rider. (#30-N-49-126, National Archives)

Below: George Armstrong Custer, reclining, with Grand Duke Alexis—who wanted a real western experience. (Library of Congress)

It was around this time, during his employment with Russell & Majors (by then Russell, Majors & Waddell), that Cody says he met "Wild Bill" Hickok, described by him as "a life-long and intimate friend of mine."

Cody's early years in the Civil War were spent as a Union scout against the Comanche and Kiowa tribes, and then the Kansas Redlegs, an abolitionist militia that stole horses and burned down farms. "We were the biggest thieves on record," Cody said. He later joined a regular Union Army unit, the Seventh Kansas Cavalry and, he says, again had adventures with Wild Bill.

And Cody did take part in the 1869 Summit Springs battle, the largest of his Indian campaigns, but he probably did not, as he proclaimed later, personally dispatch the Cheyenne chief Tall Bull. He said he retrieved

the chief's fine horse, and told his weeping widow, in her language, "that henceforth I should call the gallant steed 'Tall Bull' in honor of her husband." But Cody did not speak Cheyenne, and his changing accounts don't gel with other contemporary versions.

A drawing from the *Wild West* show depicts Cody stabbing Tall Bull; other illustrations show him shooting the hapless warrior from a ravine.

In 1876, Cody finally embarked on the work that gave him his name, shooting buffalo to feed construction crews on the Kansas Pacific Railroad. Cody claimed to have killed 4,280 of the animals in seventeen months. And when the son of the tsar of Russia, Grand Duke Alexis (just twenty-two at the time), came to the prairie to shoot buffalo, Cody and George Armstrong Custer were his chosen guides. The three were even photographed together. Cody, with his theatrical flair, brought in one hundred Indians to give the Grand Duke's hunt the proper setting.

By this time Cody had a distinct double life, taking parts in plays (often as himself) in the winter, and scouting in the summers. He was still often seen wearing his stage clothes in the field. In 1879, when Cody was thirty-three, he published a considerably embellished autobiography. It opens, "My *debut* upon the world's stage occurred on February 26th, 1845." Even that was in error, because he was actually born in 1846. In the book, Cody claims to have shot his first Indian to death in 1857, at age eleven.

Cody lived until 1917, which was long after the frontier was gone and automobiles were replacing wagons. In 1905, the legendary warrior Geronimo was photographed wearing a top hat and at the wheel of a Locomobile.

Buffalo Bill was always posing, even when out scouting. (Wikipedia)

Above: A typically florid Buffalo Bill poster. (Library of Congress)

Opposite: George Armstrong Custer, in full regalia. (Library of Congress)

In keeping with the times, Cody even became a movie producer, and trumpeted the virtues of his documentary *The Indian Wars*: "As a Money-Maker this film is without an equal. The Advertising Possibilities of the picture are unlimited. It is a FIVE-REEL THRILLER THAT WILL LIVE FOREVER," read a 1914 ad in *Moving Picture World*. Alas, no. Despite his starring role as the hero of Summit Springs and Warbonnet Creek, the film was a box-office failure.

Later filmmakers, of course, would make piles of money with wildly imaginative movies about the colorful life of Buffalo Bill. Paul Newman played the great showman in his later days for director Robert Altman. Reminded that "there's no business like show business," Newman/Cody replies gleefully, "Ain't that different from real life."

Cody lost the fortune he'd made from the Wild West show, partly through bad investments (a fate that also laid his admirer Mark Twain low). He lost the show itself in 1913, though he continued to tour in other companies.

But Cody did have a pretty good last act: helping found the town of Cody, Wyoming, in the 1890s. He had partners, but Cody himself was on the hook for most of the expenses. "For the better part of a decade, a river of money ran from Buffalo Bill's Wild West to the Big Horn Basin, scraping canals between river and settlers, building dams and headgates, erecting pumps, office buildings, stores and liveries," according to Louis Warren's *Buffalo Bill's America*.

The death of Custer, dramatically portrayed. (Library of Congress)

BUFFALO BILL'S WILD WEST

The first *Wild West* show was opened in 1883 by Bill Cody and his dentist partner Dr. W.F. Carver (who doubled as an exhibition shooter). According to the Buffalo Bill Center of the West, it wasn't a new idea—in the sixteenth century, fifty Brazilian Indians were brought to France to populate a replica of their native village. Royal visitors could observe their exotic habits from elevated walkways.

Much later, the so-called medicine shows not only employed blackface minstrels to bring the crowds in and sell their patent cures, but also buckskin-garbed "frontiersmen" and Indians in feathers. Wild Bill Hickok himself was part of a staged "buffalo hunt" at Niagara Falls in 1872. Meanwhile, Cody was putting on "border drama" plays that included the kind of frontier spectacle that later made the *Wild West* famous.

How incredible it would be to revisit the *Wild West* show today—a vanished world, like the vaudeville shows that once entranced generations of Americans. Cody's bill of fare included tableau scenes—kind of like living paintings—roping, shooting (by Annie Oakley if you were lucky, or maybe other greats like May Lillie or Lillian Smith), trick horsemanship, Pony Express rides, and the famous stagecoach raid. All of it was narrated by a skilled orator, who must have had leather lungs to drown out the cowboy band and reach the cheap seats in those days before microphones.

Of course, there were melodramas taken from history, including "Custer's Last Fight" at the Little Big Horn (and then Cody taking "the first scalp" for him). Custer's widow, Elizabeth, saw the show in 1888 and proclaimed its "terrible" realism. Sometimes Indians who were actually at the battle took the stage.

At its height, the *Wild West* employed hundreds of people and generated expenses of four thousand dollars a day. It moved around the country on railroad sleeping cars, covering eleven thousand miles in 1899 alone, and even had its own fire department. The troupe was a familiar sight in Europe, and entertained royalty.

Soon after the turn of the century, the moving pictures, including the spectacular *Great Train Robbery* of 1903, began to take its toll on Cody's enterprise and other western-themed stage shows. The *Wild West* went bankrupt in 1913, and Bill Cody went—unsuccessfully—into the film business.

Again, showmanship mingled with the sound of hammers and saws. Delegations from the town of Cody marched in Wild West parades, encouraging showgoers to visit or even settle in the Big Horn Basin. Cody thought the town would provide him some security in retirement, though that was not to be. The great scout and showman died broke, living at his sister's house in Denver.

Amusingly, Cody himself expressed public doubts about the historical record—when it came to Davy Crockett. He writes in *Story of the Old West and Fireside Chats* (1888), "The life of Crockett is accessible in an elaborate work written by his own hand, though this autobiography has been furbished up and garnished with not a few unsubstantial tales that, despite their frequent exposure, still cling tenaciously to nearly all his biographies."

Today, Buffalo Bill's legend is as big as ever, despite all we know about the historical record. And Cody, Wyoming, is thriving, thanks to housing not only the Buffalo Bill Center of the West (with five museums), but also Old Trail Town, where visitors can see the grave of the celebrated mountain man John "Liver-Eating" Johnston.

VISITING CODY

It wasn't all that easy to get to Bill Cody's namesake town in Wyoming back in the day, but it's simple enough now—it's fifty-two miles east of the famous Yellowstone Park, at the intersection of US 14-16-20 and Wyoming 120. You can also fly into the Yellowstone Regional Airport. Really, you can't miss it.

The **Buffalo Bill Center of the West** is one of the largest museums in the US, with a third of a million square feet of exhibition space. You can see western art in the **Whitney Gallery**, guns galore in the **Cody Firearms Museum**, and a huge Native American collection at the **Plains Indian Museum**. The **Draper Museum of Natural History** encourages exploration of the Greater Yellowstone ecosystem. And, of course, it's the go-to site for memorabilia related to Buffalo Bill himself (9,300 items, including the great man's Springfield buffalo gun, branding irons, and a chuck wagon from his ranch). The Center is also the place to see **Dan Miller's Cowboy Music Revue**.

A great place to stay is the **Irma Hotel**, built by Cody himself in 1902 and named after his daughter. A highlight is the French-made cherrywood backbar presented to Cody by Queen Victoria. If you want some western action, the streets next to the Irma come alive annually (June through September) with a free outdoor theatrical put on by the Gunfighters and featuring such characters as Wild Bill Hickok, Ike Clanton, "Mad Dog" Harry Tracy, Emmet Dalton, Crazy Cora, and more. The players are volunteers, but the costumes are authentic.

Cody Trolley Tours take an hour and cover twenty-two miles of historic sites and scenic vistas, via two narrators and pass-around relics. Cody is big on rodeo, and from June through August there's the only seven-days-a-week rodeo in the US. Once a year, there's the gala **Cody Fourth of July Stampede Rodeo** event, July 1–4.

Don't miss the May-to-September **Old Trail Town**, because that's where both Cody and John "Liver-Eating" Johnston are buried. Also on site are cabins used by Butch Cassidy and the Sundance Kid; and Curley, Indian scout to General Custer at the Battle of the Little Big Horn. The River Saloon was a hangout for gold miners, outlaws, and cowboys—and the bullet holes to prove it are still there.

Finally, a real novelty not available anywhere else is the recently added **Cody Dug Up Gun Museum**, featuring old iron from many historical periods, including the Gold Rush, the Old West, the Indian Wars, and even World War II. In most parts of America, digging is more likely to yield rusty tin cans than firearms, but Cody was a shoot-'em-up town.

The Buffalo Bill Center of the West in Cody, Wyoming. (Wikipedia)

WHAT HE SAID

"It was because of my great interest in the West, and my belief that its development
would be assisted by the interest I could awaken in others, that I decided to bring
the West to the East through the medium of the Wild West Show.... You who live
your lives in cities or among peaceful ways cannot always tell whether your friends are
the kind who would go through fire for you. But on the Plains one's friends have an
opportunity to prove their mettle."

*Buffalo Bill, full of
years. (Library of
Congress)*

CATHAY WILLIAMS

FIRST BLACK WOMAN

IN THE ARMY

CATHAY WILLIAMS

The only known photograph of Cathay Williams, and it may not even be her. (Wikipedia)

THE LEGEND

Cathay Williams was the only woman to serve as a Buffalo Soldier. By passing as a man ("William Cathey"), she served as a private in the all-black 38th US Infantry from 1866 to 1868.

Approximately six thousand so-called Buffalo Soldiers served in six infantry and two cavalry regiments of African-American troops in the post–Civil War army. Some twenty-three received the Medal of Honor for service during the Indian Wars. William Leckie's 1967 *Buffalo Soldiers* reports that black cavalrymen had a very low desertion rate, and fewer courts-martial for drunkenness than white soldiers. An oddity is that the 25th Regiment of black soldiers was chosen to test out the use of the recently invented safety bicycle—carrying fifty-nine-pound packs.

Williams wasn't the first American woman to enlist in the military in disguise. There are cases from the Revolutionary War, such as Deborah Sampson Gannett, who served the American cause as Robert Shirtliffe for seventeen months, and was even wounded at West Point.

And during the Civil War there was three-times-wounded "Jack Williams" (actually Frances Clalin), "Franklin Flint Thompson" (Sarah Edmonds), "Samuel 'Sammy' Blalock" (Sarah Pritchard), and even Irish-born "Albert Cashier" (Jennie Hodgers), who continued living as a man after the war. But Williams was the first documented black woman to enlist in the army, and maybe the last until the military was desegregated in 1948.

HOW THEY GET IT WRONG

There are many ballads, such as "Female Drummer" and "The Cruel War," about women passing as men to enter military service—usually to be near their true love. In Williams's case, the motives were much more practical—life was hard for former slaves during and after the Civil War. Fugitive slaves were declared "contraband of war," and often forced into serving the military. An 2015 article on Williams by Henry Louis Gates Jr. and Julie Wolf in *The Root* claims that she was indeed born a slave in 1844 (other sources say 1842), and "fled her master's plantation in Jefferson City in 1861."

Many of the songs about early female soldiers defy credibility, because it seems that the women's ruses would be easily revealed. But the real-life Williams wasn't discovered for two years, and then only because she got repeatedly sick and the truth was discovered during a medical exam.

Some accounts of Williams turn her into a pioneering figure, both for women in the military and for African-American advancement, and she was certainly admirable in finding a truly unconventional way to getting ahead. But she lived most of her life in obscurity, and would probably be astounded to find she is well remembered today.

Possibly because most Wild West/Civil War lore excludes women and black characters (at least until recently), there's not much on the record—correct or incorrect—about Cathay Williams. She'd certainly be a good subject for a film. There *is* a pretty bad cowboy poem about her. "Because of her illegal enlistment her pension passed her by," it says. "But she picked herself up and moved on/And never questioned why."

Actually, Williams definitely *did* question why. She fought hard for medical assistance in her later years, when disabled with diabetes and neuralgia.

WHAT WE ACTUALLY KNOW

Much is conjecture about Cathay Williams. According to Bruce A. Glasrud's *Buffalo Soldiers in the West: A Black Soldiers Anthology*, "Nothing is known of this woman prior to her enlistment in the U.S. Army." Glasrud claims we don't know whether she was born free or a slave, or the reason for her masquerade, but in 1876 a reporter for the *St. Louis Daily Times* got wind of Williams's story, traveled to visit her in Colorado, and in the subsequent interview addressed both issues.

The account is called "She Fought Nobly: The Story of a Colored Heroine who Served as a Regularly Enlisted Soldier During the Late War." Williams recounts, "My Father was a freeman, but my mother a slave, belonging to William Johnson, a wealthy farmer who lived at the time I was born near Independence."

Williams says her mother died there, and when the Civil War broke out she was taken to Little Rock, Arkansas, by then-colonel Thomas Hart Benton Jr. (whose uncle was the famous US Senator of the same name) of the 13th Army Corps. "I did not want to go," the account says. "He wanted me to cook for the officers, but I had always been a house girl and did not know how to cook. I learned to cook after going to Little Rock . . ."

So, after the war was over, why did Williams actually join the army that she'd lately served? "I wanted to make my own living and not be dependent on relations or friends," she said.

A US Army biographical entry on Williams records this:

> She informed her recruiting officer that she was a 22-year-old cook.
> He described her as five-foot nine, with black eyes, black hair and black
> complexion. An army surgeon examined Cathay and determined the recruit
> was fit for duty, thus sealing her fate in history as the first documented
> black woman to enlist in the Army even though U.S. Army regulations
> forbade the enlistment of women. She was assigned to the 38th U.S.
> Infantry and traveled throughout the West with her unit.

She enlisted on November 15, 1866, telling the St. Louis recruitment officer that she was from Independence, Missouri. She was illiterate, so the "Cathay" became "Cathey" on the form, and that's the name she served under. Her career was not remarkable—until she was discharged, the army singled her out neither for praise or condemnation.

Williams's masquerade was not discovered until 1868, even after several hospitalizations. Until February of 1867 she was stationed at Jefferson Barracks in Missouri, training and taking part in camp life. The first of her hospital stays occurred during this time. In April of 1867, she was sent to Fort Riley, Kansas, and soon after was again in the hospital, complaining of an itch, and was off duty until May. If doctors examined her, they didn't do it all that closely—she was in four hospitals a total of five times without being uncovered.

Williams's company marched to New Mexico's Fort Bayard in June of that year, so she must have been well enough to travel. Glasrud writes, "It appears that William Cathey withstood the marches as well as any man in her unit." Although her company scouted for signs of hostile Indians at this time, there's no record of it actually fighting.

It's interesting that Williams says in her newspaper interview that, while "I was never put in the guard house, [and] no bayonet was ever put to my back," she became bored with guard duty and other routine work. "Finally I got tired and wanted to get off," she said. "I played sick, complained of pains in my side, and rheumatism in my knees."

Considering the risk of exposure, this seems to have been a questionable strategy. And, indeed, she says, the post surgeon eventually discovered she was a woman. "The men all wanted to get rid of me after they found out I was a woman," she said. "Some of them acted real bad to me."

Discharge came in October of 1868, while "Private William Cathey" was still in New Mexico. In her "Certificate of Disability for Discharge," her commanding officer states that the soldier (referred to as a "he") was unable to work for sixty days in the last two months. Williams is described by as "feeble both physically and mentally, and much of the time quite unfit for duty. The origin of his infirmities is unknown to me."

Left: Soldiers of the Fourth United States Colored Infantry at Fort Lincoln in 1865. (Wikipedia)

Below: "The Storming of Fort Wagner," by Kurz and Allison, 1890. African-American troops fought valiantly in the Civil War, as depicted in the movie Glory. (Wikipedia)

AFRICAN-AMERICAN UNITS IN THE CIVIL WAR

President Lincoln signed the Emancipation Proclamation on the first day of 1863, and among its provisions was that African-American men "of suitable condition will be received into the armed service of the United States."

The first person killed in the Revolutionary War was a black man, Crispus Attucks, and the navy had serving African-Americans. Informal army units had been formed, but the service had always formally denied entry to men of color. That changed quickly. The History Channel reports that on February of 1863, one thousand men responded to the state's call for the 54th Massachusetts Infantry Regiment. A white officer, Robert Gould Shaw, was chosen to lead them.

In July of that year, the 54th led a desperate attack on Fort Wagner, which guarded South Carolina's Port of Charleston. The Confederate troops outnumbered the attackers by more than two to one, and almost half of the men of the 54th were killed (including their leader, Colonel Shaw).

These events form the plot of the 1989 film *Glory*, with Matthew Broderick as Shaw. In this case at least, Hollywood resisted the temptation to, well, glorify events—when the smoke clears, the Confederate flag is still flying over Fort Wagner, and white bodies lie with black.

Originally, the army was separate and very unequal. White soldiers' pay was three dollars a week more, and often they received a clothing allowance denied to blacks. That changed in 1864, when Congress decreed equal pay for all who served.

When the war ended, in 1865, a tenth of the army was black, and 180,000 men—half of them former slaves—had served. Some forty thousand black troops died, ten thousand in battle and a horrifying thirty thousand from a combination of primitive medicine and unsanitary battlefield conditions.

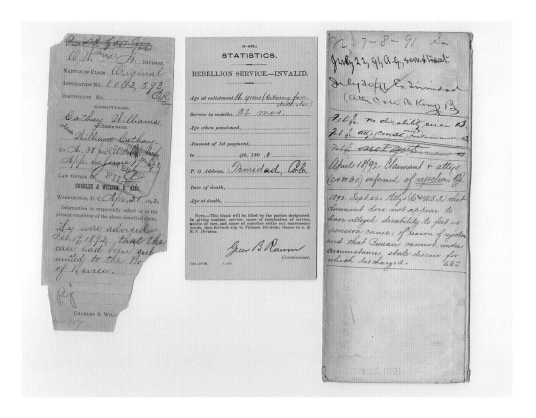

Cathay Williams (alias William Cathay) pension documents. (Wikipedia)

If the faint document is read correctly, Williams is also described by the camp surgeon as "scrofulous," which can mean "morally contaminated and corrupt." The surgeon adds, "He is continually on sick report without benefit." The notation that "this condition dates prior to enlistment" probably had repercussions for her later.

Williams wasn't much of a soldier, but certainly observed some colorful military adventures. She told the St. Louis newspaper she

> was with the Army at the Battle of Pea Ridge. Afterwards the command moved over various portions of Arkansas and Louisiana. I saw the soldiers burn lots of cotton and was at Shreveport when the rebel gunboats were captured and burned on Red River. We afterwards went to New Orleans, then by way of the Gulf to Savannah, Georgia, then to Macon and other places in the South. Finally, I was sent to Washington City and at the time General Sheridan made his raids in the Shenandoah Valley I was cook and washerwoman for his staff. I was sent from Virginia to some place in Iowa and afterwards to Jefferson Barracks [in Missouri], where I remained some time.

The Battle of Pea Ridge was in 1862, and Williams didn't enlist until 1866, but before she became a private the female version of Cathay Williams worked as a cook and laundress for several Civil War–era Union infantries. Gates and Wolf write that "records place her in Indiana, Arkansas [where the Battle of Pea Ridge occurred], Louisiana, Virginia and Georgia." General Phillip Sheridan's Virginia raids were in 1864, as was the Red River Campaign. That's all consistent with her account, as is the statement that her travels led to Jefferson Barracks near St. Louis, which is where she later enlisted.

It's hardly unknown for Civil War veterans to exaggerate their experiences, but there's no clear evidence that Williams did. She certainly did not glorify what happened to her after the army. She cooked for a colonel at Fort Union in New Mexico, then went to Pueblo, Colorado and again worked as a laundress.

Williams also got married, but describes her husband as "no account," and said he stole all her money, her watch, and a team of horses. "I had him arrested and put in jail," she said, undeterred. "I expect to get rich yet," she added, pointing out she had a sewing machine and knew how to use it. She was still determined to "not be a burden to my friends or relatives."

WOMEN WHO PASSED AS MILITARY MEN

The legend of *Mulan* aside, history teaches us that many women have disguised their gender to join the military, and many distinguished themselves in battle.

Joan of Arc dressed as a man to lead the French army to victory over the English during the Hundred Years' War in the fifteenth century. She died—burned at the stake as a heretic—when she was only nineteen.

Elisa Bernerström joined the Swedish army during the Finnish War between Sweden and Russia (1808 and 1809). She wanted to be near her serving husband—a frequently cited explanation for female soldiers in popular ballads. Bernerström served in the Queen's Regiment, but was eventually discovered—and also cited for bravery in battle.

During the Mexican War of 1846-1848, Elizabeth Newcom enlisted in the Missouri Volunteer Infantry as "Bill Newcom" and marched some six hundred miles to winter camp in Colorado before her ruse was uncovered.

Sarah Rosetta is another woman who served in the Civil War—as Lyons Wakeman. She was escaping her family's debts and a lack of marriage prospects. In the 153rd New York infantry, she camped in Virginia and Washington, DC, and then saw action in Louisiana. Letters from her survive and are published in her book *An Uncommon Soldier*. "I don't know how long before I shall have to go in the field of battle," the tobacco-chewing Rosetta wrote. "For my part I don't care. I don't feel afraid to go . . . I am as independent as a hog on the ice."

Rosetta was in Louisiana at the Battle of Pleasant Hill in 1864. She wrote, "There was a heavy cannonading [*sic*] all day and a sharp firing of infantry. I had to face the enemy bullets with my regiment. I was under fire about four hours and laid on the field of battle all night." Rosetta wasn't killed by enemy fire, though, she was taken down—as were so many Civil War casualties—by disease. She contracted chronic dysentery after a forced march. Amazingly, Rosetta's ruse was never discovered, despite (like Williams) going through long periods of medical care. She died an "honest" and "faithful" soldier.

Reports *Time* magazine, "Had Rosetta lived, she may well have spent the rest of her days as a man, as multiple women actually did when the fighting was over." There aren't many reports of women passing as military men in the twentieth century. Perhaps that's because medical care had gotten better, and the masquerade was harder to sustain.

Williams might have faded from public view at this point, but instead she reentered it in 1891, when, still in Colorado, she filed for an invalid pension based on her military service. That must have taken chutzpah, because here was a woman asking for a pension that was due to a man.

But there was precedent—the aforementioned Deborah Sampson Gannett received both state and military pensions— in part because of the personal intervention of Paul Revere. Mary Hayes McCauley and Margaret Corbin, both nicknamed "Molly Pitcher" for their Revolutionary War service (a prime duty was carrying water to the troops), were also pensioned. The latter pair didn't pose as men, though.

Sarah Rosetta Wakeman as Private Lyons Wakeman. (Wikipedia)

Williams claimed she was suffering from deafness (brought on by smallpox), rheumatism, and neuralgia, and could no longer do manual labor. She gave her age as forty-one, but if she was born in 1844 it was forty-seven. When a doctor examined her later in 1891 as part of the claim, he said she was large, stout, and forty-nine. He also reported she'd lost all the toes on both feet, and could hardly walk. In 1892, the pension claim was rejected, and Cathay Williams faded from view. She may have died before 1900, but one researcher claims to have found records of her working as a dressmaker in Colorado as late as 1910. Maybe that sewing machine came in handy after all.

WHAT SHE SAID

From Williams's account in the *St. Louis Daily Times* in 1876: "The regiment I joined wore the Zouave uniform and only two persons, a cousin and a particular friend, members of the regiment, knew I was a woman. They never 'blowed' on me."

JAMES BECKWOURTH

A LOT OF IT WAS

ACTUALLY TRUE

JAMES BECKWOURTH

James Beckwourth told some tall tales, but his life was definitely colorful. (Wikipedia)

THE LEGEND

James Beckwourth, of mixed race, was a blacksmith, trapper, mountain man, soldier (in the second Seminole War in Florida), Indian expert (he lived with the Crow Nation for years, spoke the language, and married among them), superb Indian fighter (with the unique approach of fighting one tribe while ensconced in another), and a talented explorer. The Beckwourth Pass through the Sierra Nevadas is named after him, as is the Beckwourth Trail, a route for early settlers to California. His autobiography is the only one from an African-American in the West. If his name doesn't trip off the tongue along with that of Kit Carson or Jim Bridger, that may be because the role of black men and women is frequently written out of western history.

HOW THEY GET IT WRONG

It starts with his name, which is variously reported as Beckwourth, Beckworth and (after his father) Beckwith. Beckwourth was known for telling "monumental tales of his exploits, some true, some embellished in mountain man style," as *American Heritage* describes it. Many of these stories made it into his autobiography—as fact.

Between 1854 and 1855, Beckwourth dictated *James P. Beckwourth: Mountaineer, Scout, Pioneer and Chief of the Crow Nation* to Thomas D. Bonner, an itinerant justice of the peace and a former temperance preacher who, according to Peter Fish in *Sunset* magazine, "had fallen noisily off the wagon." The process was colorful: "Beckwourth dictated, Bonner transcribed, both drank—each shot of rum increasing the number of enemies Beckwourth had slain and the number of Indian maidens who had found his charms irresistible. 'Paint her up, Bonner,' Beckwourth would shout."

It might have been better if Bonner didn't "paint 'er up" quite so much, because Beckwourth was an impressive figure without the embellishment. Fish describes him as "six feet tall, with dark hair that coiled to his waist—he was one of those figures who swagger even when standing still."

Susan Gregson's *James Beckwourth: Mountaineer, Scout and Pioneer* reports that it may have been Bonner who changed Beckwith's name to Beckwourth—"or perhaps it was just another spelling error on Bonner's part." Bonner tended to render phonetically any name he got from Beckwourth orally. But you'd think he could at least get straight the spelling of his subject's name.

Given the provenance, it's amusing that the preface to the 1892 English edition of Beckwourth's book, written by American humorist Charles Godfrey Leland, takes aim at dime novels and "cheap romances of the 'Scalp Hunter' and 'Bandits of the Plains' description," and informs us how lucky we are to be hearing from a real wilderness voice.

But Leland adds, "That Beckwourth had the very general frontier weakness of spinning marvelous yarns, and that he seldom narrated an adventure without making the utmost of it, even when it was perfectly needless, is probably true." But Leland is careful to add that the truth was probably just as fantastic. "He had, beyond all question, undergone hundreds of adventures as wild and characteristic as any described in this book."

So the book is true—not to what actually happened, but to the spirit of James Beckwourth, storyteller. Leland again, "The reader may be perfectly assured of the truth of every word of these reminiscences, and it is evident that they correspond altogether to the manner and style of adventure narrated by Beckwourth himself."

The autobiography, which its modern editor, Bernard DeVoto, says is not history nor fiction but mythology, found an audience, including in Europe. The book starts this way.

> Among the many men who have distinguished themselves as mountaineers, traders, chiefs of great Indian nations, and as early pioneers in the settlement of our Pacific coast, is James P. Beckwourth, whose varied and startling personal adventures would have found no record but for the accident of meeting with a wanderer in the mountains of California, interested in the man, and, patiently listening to his story, proceeded, as it fell from his lips, to put it upon paper. This autobiography was thus produced, and was the result of some months' labor in the winter of 1854–55.

How much was true? The stories may have fallen from Beckwourth's lips, but that was no guarantee they were even in the same room as what actually happened. Beckwourth's acquaintances apparently took his book as a collection of whoppers.

A website dedicated to this pioneering mountain man, Beckwourth.org, notes, "For the early fur trappers of the Rockies, the ability to 'spin a good yarn' was a skill valued almost as highly as marksmanship or woodmanship." The site says Beckwourth "had a tendency to exaggerate numbers or to occasionally make himself the hero of events that happened to other people." Nevertheless, the site claims that "later historians have discovered that much of what Beckwourth related in his autobiography actually occurred."

Contemporaries doubted it. A group of miners gathered to have the book read to them, but the careless reader picked up a Bible by mistake and read the group the account of Samson and the foxes. "That'll do," a miner cried. "That'll do! I'd know that story for one of Jim Beckwourth's lies anywhere!"

An African-American character possibly based on Beckwourth appears in *The Revenant* film, but there's no evidence that he knew Hugh Glass (they served in the same outfit, but at different times). Beckwourth did claim to have been in the party that buried Glass in 1833, but that account is doubted. Beckwourth is also enshrined on a twenty-nine-cent stamp issued in 1994.

JAMES P. BECKWOURTH
AN EARLY CALIFORNIAN FAMOUS AS TRAPPER AND SCOUT

James Beckwourth in pioneer garb. (Wikipedia)

WHAT WE ACTUALLY KNOW

Beckwourth had a white father, reportedly an authentic nobleman, Sir Jennings Beckwith, and a slave mother, possibly Catherine Miskell. He says he was one of thirteen children; the Beckwith genealogy says eleven. He says his birth date in Virginia was 1798, but some historians say 1800. Beckwourth was legally a slave, but was recognized as a son by his father.

According to the autobiography, Jennings Beckwith served in the Revolutionary War as a major. "I well recollect, when a small boy, the frequent meetings of the old patriots at my father's house, who would sit down and relate the different battles in which they had taken part during 'those days that tried men's souls,'" the autobiography relates. But Sir Jennings Beckwith was born between 1760 and 1765, and that would likely have make him too young to be a major in the War of Independence.

Beckwourth's father moved the family to St. Louis, and apprenticed his son to a blacksmith. According to *True West*, when young James was in his early twenties, his father executed a Deed of Emancipation to the "mulatto boy," granting him freedom.

Beckwourth had the urge to travel, and managed to convince his father to let him leave his apprenticeship. "He gave me five hundred dollars in cash, together with a good horse, saddle and bridle, and bade me God speed upon my journey," according to the autobiography. In 1824, Beckwourth signed on with General William Ashley's fur company to handle the horses on a trip into the Rockies. All of his great adventures stem from this new life as a trapper and mountain man.

"If everything in Beckwourth's autobiography can be believed, he played a leading role in virtually every recorded event in the Rocky Mountains in the late 1820s," reports a biography at Beckwourth.org. But as the questions about his birth date make clear, the great mountain man played fast and loose—including with numbers (such as his birth date). "If 50 trappers were attacked by 50 Blackfeet, Beckwourth might report 10 trappers attacked by 500 Blackfeet," the biography says. "And, of course, it was always Beckwourth's skill and bravery that saved the day."

BECKWOURTH AS AN INDIAN WARRIOR.

Beckwourth in his Indian attire. (Wikipedia)

Beckwourth, with General Ashley, took part in the first of the Mountain Man Rendezvous events at Henry's Fork on the Green River in 1825. And he was acquainted with such leading colleagues as Jim Bridger (Beckwourth says he was "as skilful a hunter as ever lived in the mountains"—Bridger also discovered the Great Salt Lake and a passage through the Rockies known as Bridger's Pass); and the aforementioned Jedediah Smith, who reportedly taught him the fur business.

Smith, who was also noted among his contemporaries for taking regular baths, became Ashley's partner in the fur trade. He was probably the most well-traveled mountain man, becoming the first American to visit California by way of the Southwest and the Mojave Desert. He was also the first to cross the Sierra Nevadas from the west.

Beckwourth depicts himself as a fierce Indian fighter. In one conflict with the scalp-taking Blackfeet—thirty of his party against five hundred Indians, he writes,

> On our side we lost four men killed and seven wounded. Not a woman or child was injured. From the enemy we took 17 scalps. . . . We were satisfied they had more than a hundred slain; but as they always carry off their dead, we could not ascertain the exact number. We also lost two packs of beavers, a few packs of meat, together with some valuable horses. . . . I now began to deem myself Indian-proof, and to think I never should be killed by them.

Why were the fights so lopsided, even against warriors as fierce as the Blackfeet? Beckwourth says it's because they were poor marksmen with rifles, and had to be close to fire their arrows accurately.

Beckwourth was a lover as well as a fighter. The mountain man had "a long string of 'affairs of the heart,' although pragmatism seemed to be more of a driving force than his heart," the biography said. This was despite Eliza, the woman he left behind in St. Louis. When they parted, Beckwourth reported, "I left her amid her sobs, promising to make a speedy return, and that we would part no more till death should separate us." He knew that "her fond heart beat alone for me," but none of this stopped him from repeatedly marrying others.

While a guest of the Blackfeet (later his sworn enemies) Beckwourth became close to their head chief, As-as-to, who offered his daughter's hand in marriage. Soon after, he brained her with a battle ax, after she supposedly danced joyously to celebrate the taking of three white scalps. As-as-to doesn't hold this against Beckwourth, agreed she deserved it, and offered another, prettier daughter. "I found her, as her father had represented, far more intelligent and far prettier than her other sister, and I was really proud of the change," said Beckwourth. Neither marriage lasted long, as the mountain man was soon on his way.

Beckwourth definitely did live seven or eight years among the warlike Crows, after being captured by them while on a trapping expedition in 1825. His situation was helped by fact that he was "recognized" as Morning Star, the long-lost son of warrior Big Bowl (later, he's known as Medicine Calf). Some sources say Beckwourth wasn't captured by the Crows, but went to stay with them to further trade on behalf of his fur company employer. *The Complete Encyclopedia of African-American History* says he was fleeing a debt collector.

JAMES P. BECKWOURTH IN CITIZEN'S DRESS.

James Beckwourth in western finery. He thrived in two worlds. (Wikipedia)

Beckwourth says he didn't see a white man for three years. In his account, he became a revered figure in the tribe—eventually, head chief—because of the many successful raids he led against other Indians. "They began to associate my name with victory," he said. Undoubtedly some of what Beckwourth said about his life with the Crows actually happened, because there's some outside documentation, but undoubtedly at a lower level of violence and personal heroism than in the autobiographical accounts (which take up more than half of his book).

In one encounter with the Blackfeet, Beckwourth claimed to have taken 170 scalps, "besides an abundance of weapons, baggage and horses." His Crows suffered twenty-nine wounded. For the battle, he wore "a superb headdress, ornamented with eagles' feathers and weasels' tails"—and three of the tails were severed by a Blackfoot bullet that grazed the mighty warrior's scalp. On two occasions, bullets bounce harmlessly off his big hunting knife. In a later scrape, Beckwourth's troops dispatch ninety-one Blackfeet. The number of scalps (mostly from Blackfeet) taken in Beckwourth's telling is positively breathtaking. It's easy to imagine how he told these tales to an enraptured throng.

And while in the Crow camp Beckwourth married Still-water, the daughter of a "great Crow brave." Beckwourth says she lived up to her name. "She was affectionate, obedient, gentle, cheerful, and, apparently, quite happy," he wrote. "No domestic thunderstorms, no curtain-lectures ever disturbed the serenity of our connubial lodge." Soon he had eight wives—maybe as many as ten—and a lodge for each. Children were born. Beckwourth reports that one of his sons was first counselor of the Crow Nation in 1855.

The last marriage was to the fierce Pine Leaf ("she seemed incapable of fear"), who fought alongside him. Pine Leaf's twin brother was killed by the Blackfeet, and she swore she wouldn't get married until she'd taken one hundred of their scalps, though she finally succumbed to the mountain man's charms. But Beckwourth seemed to have no trouble loving and leaving; he admitted their stay together was only five weeks, and "I have never seen her since.")

Beckwourth described a kind of double life. He said he was both the adored leader of the Blackfeet and a trusted elder among the fur trappers—useful for keeping the Blackfeet at bay. This quote gives the flavor: "Having finished the construction of the fort, I gave full instructions for the management of its affairs, and then departed for the [Crow] village, where my presence was required to incite the Indians to devote themselves to trapping and hunting buffalo, for which service I was paid by the American Fur Company." Jim Beckwourth, a very busy king of the wild frontier.

Finally, fourteen years after he'd last seen it, Beckwourth returned to St. Louis. The fur business was declining, both because of changing fashions and over-trapping. And the endless Crow wars were trying the patience of the American Fur Company. The tribe was also much reduced by the smallpox epidemic that roared through the plains in 1837. Beckwourth was accused of having a hand in its spread, but the accusations are unlikely.

In St. Louis, Beckwourth had a tearful reunion with his sisters, Louise and Matilda, who'd thought him dead. "I must have been a curious-looking object for an affectionate sister to recognize," he wrote. "All my clothing consisted of dressed antelope, deer and the skins of mountain sheep, highly ornamented by my Indian wives. My long hair, as black as the raven's wing, descended to my hips, and I presented more the appearance of a Crow than that of a civilized being."

Eliza, alas, has married another. "She is lost to me forever!" The mourning was short, however, because he had several other marriages. Beckwourth was also reunited with General Ashley in St. Louis, and the mountain man reports him proclaiming, "This is the man that saved my life on three different occasions in the Rocky Mountains."

But Beckwourth's next adventure was far from the Rockies; while in St. Louis, he met General William Gaines, who was recruiting mountain men "familiar with Indian habits" to serve in the still-raging Second Seminole War (1835–1842) in Florida. Beckwourth said he was tired of fighting Indians, but Gaines won him over with promises of "renown." Late in 1837, Beckwourth recruited a force of sixty-four mountain men, was appointed their chief, and was paid fifty dollars a month to be an express rider and sub-conductor of the muleteers.

A contemporary image from the Second Seminole War. The hand-colored lithograph is entitled "Attack of the Seminoles on the Block House." Beckwourth joined the fray in 1837, but the costly war raged on until 1842. (Wikipedia)

In Florida, Beckwourth's primary engagement was at the Battle of Okeechobee on Christmas Day, 1837. For once, he doesn't make himself the center of events, but recounts a bloody swamp conflict between Colonel (and later President) Zachary Taylor and the Seminoles led by warriors with colorful names such as Bill Bowlegs, Abiaca, and Alligator. The Seminoles had African-American allies, and here's a flavorful passage from Beckwourth: "A Missourian picked off a fine fat negro who had ensconced

AFRICAN-AMERICAN MOUNTAIN MEN

James Beckwourth was by no means the only man of color trading furs and blazing trails on the frontier. Slavery was legal during the fur trade, and history records that a black man named Reese, a servant to Francis A. Cardon, was killed by Blackfeet at Fort Chardon at the mouth of the Judith River, somewhere between 1842 and 1845. The pioneering frontier anthropologist and artist George Catlin records the death of another unnamed slave, the property of a Judge Martin, killed by Indians in what is now Oklahoma in 1835.

Black slaves were reported (by English visitor John Palliser) at Fort Union Trading Post during 1847 and 1848, and three lived and worked at Bent's Fort on the Arkansas River. Charles Bent's slave, Charlotte, was a popular cook—not just because her food was good, but because she was one of the few non–Native American women around. Charlotte and her husband, Dick Green, were later freed after Green showed considerable courage in fighting off a force of Mexican and Pueblo Indian forces during the Taos Rebellion of 1847.

A number of free African-Americans were trappers and guides. But according to a report by William W. Gwaltney, former superintendent of the Fort Laramie National Historic Site, the information we have on them is often frustratingly scant.

Two free men, Jacob Dodson and Sanders Jackson, accompanied John C. Frémont on his 1848 California expedition. And Dodson, who worked alongside Kit Carson, also fought in the Bear Flag revolt for California independence. Peter Ranne crossed the Mojave Desert with Jedediah Smith, and may be the first black person to reach California by a land route.

George William Bush was a veteran of the Battle of New Orleans in 1814, and later rode with white companions from the Mexican border to the Columbia River—where a law said that any black person entering Oregon would be arrested and beaten. With his group vowing to protect him, Bush was not molested.

himself in a live oak tree. As he fell to the ground it shook beneath him: the fruit was ripe, but unfit for food." But Beckwourth admits that the Seminoles ultimately got the better of Taylor's troops.

In 1838, after ten months in Florida (and failing to find the renown he sought), Beckwourth was bored. "I began to grow tired of Florida. . . . It seemed to me to be a country dear even at the price of the powder to blow the Indians out of it. . . . I wanted

Edward Rose, who lived from 1780 to 1833, had a white trader father and a mother who was part Cherokee and part African-American. His early life, including his birthplace, are unknown. According to a short biography by Donald Grinde Jr. of the State University of New York at Buffalo, he may have been a riverman for a time, working the Mississippi from southern Illinois to New Orleans.

Rose, who also went by such Indian names as "Cut Nose" and "Five Scalps," spent time—as Beckwourth did—with the Crows in southern Montana and northern Wyoming. And also like Beckwourth, he learned their language and became comfortable living among them.

And Rose was similarly a fur trapper, interpreter and guide, hired in 1807 by Manuel Lisa on an excursion to the Bighorn River. Here, he probably crossed paths with Benito Vasquez. In 1809, he worked with Lisa and his partner Andrew Henry at the Knife River in current-day North Dakota, and in 1811 for John Jacob Astor's company in Crow country.

Rose lived with the Arikaras and also learned their language. In 1823, he was a guide and interpreter for William Henry Ashley's trip up the Missouri River, where he probably first met Hugh Glass. Later in 1823, he was an interpreter and guide in Colonel Henry Leavenworth's campaign against the warlike Arikara.

After that experience, Rose returned to the Crows, led war parties, and earned those Indian names (Five Scalps because he killed that many Blackfeet in a battle). Rose lived with Indians and was killed by them. In 1833, near Fort Cass, he was one of the two men the Arikaras killed with Hugh Glass.

Gwaltney describes Rose as "a notorious brigand whose life story is almost as fantastic as that of Beckwourth." Indian fighting was definitely part of the job for African-Americans on the frontier. In 1840, a black man known as Andy worked with scalpers Peg Leg Smith, James Kirker, and Shawnee Spiebuck in killing Apaches for money.

The site of Beckwourth's Battle of Lake Okeechobee, during the Second Seminole War in 1837. (Ebay.be/Wikipedia Creative Commons)

excitement of some kind." He returned to the Rockies for three years of trading missions among the Cheyenne and other tribes (mostly enemies of the Crows). The Seminoles, it seemed, didn't have any horses worth stealing.

By 1844, after some misadventures in New Mexico, Beckwourth's trading took him in 1844 to California and Pueblo de Angeles, then sleepy and Spanish, but later Los Angeles. Continuing his penchant for being where the action was, Beckwourth became embroiled in the Bear Flag Rebellion, an 1845 revolt of California's white settlers against Mexican control.

He was there at the Battle of Cahuenga Pass, but does he report events accurately? No. "He got the names all wrong," reports Beckwourth.org. "Governor Micheltorena becomes 'Torrejon,' while Rowland, one of the leaders recruiting insurgents, becomes 'Roland.' Other key leaders aren't even mentioned. And, of course, he becomes the leader and hero of every encounter."

Beckwourth also had an issue with numbers. Is it really plausible that he was able to round up an amazing "1,800 stray horses" that were roaming the California ranchos and deliver them to US troops in New Mexico after war was declared against Mexico? Soon after purchasing a hotel, he's in the thick of it again, taking revenge for a Mexican massacre of the white citizens of Taos, then avenging the savage murder of the Reed family (eleven were killed) near Monterey, California. Evidence suggests he really was involved in both things.

Beckwourth does have many genuine achievements: He gets credit for discovering Beckwourth Pass, which is now where California Route 70 crosses the Sierra Nevadas. "From some of the elevations over which we passed I remarked a place far away to the southward that seemed lower than any other. . . . I had come to discover what I suspected to be a pass. . . . I imparted my views to three of my

BECKWOURTH PUNISHES HIS DISOBEDIENT WIFE.

Beckwourth brains his wife for misconduct. According to the autobiography, the father didn't mind and offered a more obedient second daughter. (Wikipedia)

companions in whose judgment I placed the most confidence. They thought highly of the discovery, and even proposed to associate with me in opening the road." He led the first train, with seventeen wagons, through the pass that bears his name.

Again, Beckwourth's timing was uncanny. The Gold Rush was on when he arrived in California in 1848, and his second great achievement as an explorer, in 1850, was improving an old Native American path through the mountains from Pyramid Lake to Marysville and the northern California gold fields. It saved the gold hunters 150 miles of travel and a trip through the Donner Pass.

Beckwourth opened a trading post and ranch in the Sierras, catering to the miners who expected to return "with whole cart-loads of gold dust, and dazzle their neighbors' eyes with their excellent good fortune." And it was in the Sierras, where Beckwourth was ranching and running a trading post, that he ran into his biographer, Thomas Bonner.

Beckwourth was supposed to get half the profits from the book, but didn't. The autobiography's publication in 1856 did finally get him some of the renown he'd sought, since Gregson reports that "people traveled to the ranch to meet the frontiersman, who by this time was nearly 60 years old."

Beckwourth complained that he also wasn't remunerated for his work on the two invaluable trails. "Sixteen hundred dollars I expended upon the road [Beckwourth Pass] is forever gone," he wrote. "But those who derive advantage from this outlay and loss of time devote no thought to the discoverer; nor do I see clearly how I am to help myself, for everyone knows I cannot roll a mountain into the pass and shut it up." At least Marysville gave him credit, in 1996, with Beckwourth Riverfront Park.

Beckwourth ends his book, "I have now presented a plain, unvarnished statement of the most noteworthy occurrences of my life, and, in so doing, I have necessarily led the reader through a variety of savage scenes at which his heart must sicken." Actually, probably not—it's too bad Beckwourth didn't live to see the craze for cowboy-and-Indian movies and TV shows in the 1950s.

In 1859, Beckwourth pulled up stakes in California and, that same year, settled in Colorado, where he ran a store and became an Indian agent. This is, unfortunately, where his record as a friend of the Native American was stained, because he was hired by Colonel John M. Chivington of the Third Colorado Volunteers to act as scout during an offensive against the Cheyenne and Apache. The campaign's black mark was the Sand Creek massacre of 1864, resulting in the deaths of at least one hundred peace-seeking Cheyenne and Arapaho, including women and children.

Chief Black Kettle was waving an American flag as the troops charged. Nonetheless, the soldiers returned to wild acclaim, and scalps were displayed in a Denver theater.

Accounts of the killings have unpleasant parallels to the Vietnam War My Lai massacre, including a contest to see who could pick off a small Indian boy. As with My Lai, a federal inquiry was ordered. Larry McMurtry writes in *Oh What a Slaughter* that it's disputed how much of the massacre was witnessed by Beckwourth, but the old mountain man later testified against Chivington. He said that the Cheyenne and Arapahos had been friendly, and that the soldiers slaughtered them.

At the tribunal, Chivington—who was never punished—testified firmly that the war chiefs from both tribes were assembled and ready to attack, and that his actions were justified. He said,

> I believed the Indians in the camp were hostile to the whites. That they were of the same tribes with those who had murdered many persons and destroyed much valuable property . . . was beyond a doubt. When a tribe of Indians is at war with the whites, it is impossible to determine . . . the name of the Indian or Indians belonging to the tribe [who] are guilty of the acts of hostility. The most that can be ascertained is that Indians of the tribe have performed the acts.

At the end of his life, Beckwourth returned to the Rockies, worked briefly as an army scout at Fort Laramie in Wyoming, and even worked with Jim Bridger as a guide to Colonel Henry B. Carrington at Fort Kearny—and visiting the Crows again was part of the agenda. A friend of Beckwourth's, founder of the *Rocky Mountain News*, claimed he was poisoned by the Crows in 1866 because of his role in the Sand Creek Massacre—but there's no clear evidence of that. Some said that one of his many former Crow wives poisoned him, but the *Complete Encyclopedia of African-American History* discounts this, and says he died of food poisoning while on his way to a Crow encampment.

Trader Julius Mayer (upper left) with Chief Red Cloud on the frontier. (Wikipedia)

PIONEER JEWS IN THE WILD WEST

African-American and Hispanic people were not the only important players left out of popular histories and films about settling the West.

According to Harriet and Fred Rochlin's *Pioneer Jews*, a 16th-century manuscript from Cuba quoted by Friar Juan de Torquemada claims that the Western Indian languages "were rife with Yiddish and Hebrew," and that the Indian peoples bore some resemblance to Jews, both in appearance and custom. Could the lost Israelites have made their way to the New World?

Joseph Smith, founder of the Church of Jesus Christ of Latter-Day Saints, said that the golden plates he found in New York were inscribed with a *New World Bible* that had been prepared by the Israelites, and brought by them to North America. Early Mormons believed the Israelites were the first Americans.

"Jews in the Wild West" by Dr. Yvette Alt Miller reports, "America's western regions in the 1800s were home to thousands of Jews." An 1878 survey by the Union of American Hebrew Congregations—the first of its kind—found 21,465 Jews in eleven western states and territories. Here are some stories gathered by Miller:

New Yorker Flora Langerman married Willie Spiegelberg in 1874, and the pair spent their honeymoon on the Santa Fe Trail, heading for New Mexico. She reported a royal welcome in the town of Las Animas, then the terminus of the westbound trains. "'Hello, lady, glad to see you,' they shouted, and they really meant it, for I was the first woman they had laid eyes on in months.'"

In Santa Fe, Langerman started a Jewish school, and in 1884 Spiegelberg became the city's first mayor. Miller also records, in the 1860s, Jewish businessman Julius Meyer trading with the Sioux in today's Nebraska. Meyer was hunting buffalo when he was captured by the tribe, and he spent several years living with them and learning their language—as well as five other Native American tongues.

Solomon Bibo, born in Germany with a cantor father, also settled in Santa Fe, where he traded with the Acoma tribe. He became the tribe's advocate, married an Acoma woman, and became the elected leader—apparently an enlightened one—in 1885. He eventually resettled in San Francisco and lived a more conventional life.

Jews on the frontier. (Wikipedia)

Loeb (eventually Levi) Strauss was a German-Jewish immigrant who moved to California to supply dry goods to miners who were there for the Gold Rush. In 1872, working with one of his customers, he developed the first metal-riveted blue jeans. He later endowed San Francisco's first synagogue.

Josephine Sarah Marcus, known as Sadie, claimed to have been one of the few eyewitnesses to the Gunfight at the O.K. Corral in 1881. In something of a Romeo and Juliet situation, she had a past lover and a future one on opposite sides of the battle. But Marcus recalled that when she reached the scene and spotted Wyatt Earp, her only thought was, "My God, I haven't got a bonnet on. What will they think?"

That story may be apocryphal—Marcus was known to stretch the truth, and some say she wasn't even in Tombstone at that time. But meet Josephine Marcus and Wyatt Earp certainly did. And the first impression was evidently fine (Earp confederate Bat Masterson described her as "an incredible beauty"). Earp and his Sadie were together almost fifty years. Earp is buried in a Jewish cemetery.

Jim Levy was a professional gambler and gunslinger—living in such iconic locales as Cheyenne, Deadwood, Tombstone, Leadville, and Tucson. He was gunned down in Tucson after an 1882 gambling session at the Fashion Saloon. If Levy had died in Tombstone, he could have been buried in the Jewish burial ground that was established as part of Boot Hill in 1881.

A doctrinal dispute in an Orthodox congregation in Portland, Oregon, grew heated, and led to a downtown shootout in 1880 between Rabbi Moses May and synagogue president A. Waldman. The latter grabbed the former on the street in front of the Esmond Hotel, and broke his glasses. Moses responded by pulling out a pistol, and shooting wildly at Waldman. One bullet went through Waldman's coat, but then Moses was restrained before he could reload.

So there's more than one hidden history in the Old West. Jewish life on the prairie was very real, and was even parodied in the 1966 song "The Ballad of Irving."

WHAT HE SAID

Beckwourth appears to have had a far more enlightened view of Indians than most of his contemporaries, probably because he lived among them. According to his autobiography,

> I have lived among Indians in the Eastern and Western States, on the Rocky Mountains, and in California; I find their habits of living, and their religious belief, substantially uniform through all the unmingled races. All believe in the same Great Spirit; all have their prophets, their medicine men, and their soothsayers, and are alike influenced by the appearance of omens; thus leading to the belief that the original tribes throughout the entire continent, from Florida to the most northern coast, have sprung from one stock, and still retain in some degree of purity the social constitution of their primitive founders.

Beckwourth wrote,

> I learned this one truth while I was with the Indians, namely, that a white man can easily become an Indian, but that an Indian could never become a white man. Some of the very worst savages I ever saw in the Rocky Mountains were white men, and I could mention their names and expose some of their deeds, but they have most probably gone to their final account before this.

BLACK BEAVER

AN HONORABLE

SCOUT

BLACK BEAVER
(SUCK-TUM-MAH-KWAY)

Black Beaver was an honest man. (#75-ID-118A, National Archives)

THE LEGEND

Black Beaver, a Delaware born in 1806, was a trapper, farmer, and mountain man, as well as a much-in-demand guide and interpreter (he spoke English, French, Spanish, and eight Indian languages, as well as sign language) to federal troops before and after the Mexican and Civil Wars. He also escorted distinguished visitors, such as, in 1843, the naturalist John James Audubon. It's said that without him, the Chisholm Trail may have never come to be, and Oklahoma could have been lost to the Union in 1861. He was described as "one of God's noblemen, honest and truthful" by his close friend Israel G. Vore, quartermaster on the staff of General Douglas H. Cooper during the Civil War.

HOW THEY GET IT WRONG

Black Beaver led an honorable life, and showed extraordinary forbearance in the face of his tribe's considerable ill-use by both the federal and Confederate governments. If he's not better known, it's probably because he doesn't fit neatly into a patriotic narrative of heroic western expansion. Instead, his story vividly illustrates the poor treatment of Native Americans at the hands of officials armed with fountain pen and paper. It's not surprising that by the 1850s Black Beaver was described, in W. David Baird's *The Story of Oklahoma*, as "worn out by his journeys." But broken promises did not him deter from a lifetime commitment to forging peace between two very different peoples.

WHAT WE ACTUALLY KNOW

Black Beaver was born in 1806 in an Indian village that is now Belleville, Illinois, not far from St. Louis. His father was a Delaware chief, Captain William Patterson. The Delaware were then located mostly in Indiana and Cape Girardeau, Missouri.

According to Kerry Holton, president of the Delaware Nation, "Very little is known about his youth, though he was a seemingly rambunctious child. Throughout his adolescence he spent his time hunting, trapping and otherwise honing his skills in travel and survival."

Black Beaver next appears in the public record in the mid-1820s, when he is among the Delaware gathered at the Jacob Wolf House (which still stands, possibly the oldest house in the Ozarks) on the White River in Norfolk, Arkansas. Davy Crockett and Sam Houston are among the notables who reportedly visited, since the location was a gathering place for trappers, traders, and native peoples.

Early on, Black Beaver became an advocate for his people. Carolyn Thomas Foreman writes in the 1946 *Chronicles of Oklahoma* that Black Beaver was one of the authors of a letter sent to General William Clark in 1824, decrying the conditions their tribe had been reduced to after being relocated to Arkansas—and having nearly all their horses stolen by white people. "Father," they wrote, "you know it is hard to go hungry. If you do not know it, we poor Indians know it. . . . We are obliged to call on you onst more for assistance in the name of God."

According to Laurence M. Hauptman in *Between Two Fires*, Black Beaver was "by far the most accomplished Indian scout before the Civil War." In 1834, then twenty-eight, he became a guide and interpreter for General Henry Leavenworth and Colonel Richard Dodge during councils with the Comanche, Kiowa, and Wichita Indians on the Upper Red River. He was employed by John Jacob Astor's American Fur Company—as James Beckwourth was—during the 1830s and 1840s.

In 1846, during the Mexican-American War, Black Beaver went to San Antonio and organized, then commanded, a volunteer company of Delaware and Shawnee Indians

Black Beaver in later years, burdened by mistreatment. (Wikipedia)

that served ably under General William S. Harney for several months. In a later letter asking for reparations, he wrote, "I have been in the employ of the Government all, or nearly all the time since the commencement of the Mexican war."

After this, by his own later testimony, Black Beaver was employed as a guide and interpreter by a variety of commanders at Fort Cobb and Arbuckle in the Indian Territory, and also as superintendent and agent for the Indians in the vicinity. He said he was at Fort Arbuckle for five years, and Fort Cobb for one year "immediately preceding the last [Civil] war."

Black Beaver was initially a guide for trappers, but when that trade declined in the 1840s he became an invaluable leader of wagon trains headed west, as well as trailblazer for luminaries such as the aforementioned Audubon. Starting from Fort Smith, Arkansas, in 1849, he led a group of five hundred emigrants under William Randolph Marcy, a Civil War general and explorer of the Southwest, to Santa Fe. The route the group laid out became known as the Marcy Trail, and was later adopted by the Butterfield Overland Mail. By 1853, Black Beaver had reportedly seen the Pacific Ocean seven times.

Marcy's diaries of that period say that Black Beaver

> visited nearly every point of interest within the limits of our unsettled territory. He had set his traps and spread his blanket upon the headwaters of the Missouri and Columbia; and his wanderings had led him south of the Colorado and Gila, and thence to the shores of the Pacific in Southern California. His life is that of a veritable cosmopolite, filled with scenes of intense and startling interest, bold and reckless adventure.

He was, Marcy said, "the great Delaware," a "resolute, determined and fearless warrior . . . yet I have never seen a man who wore his laurels with less vanity."

Black Beaver's services were particularly valuable because he was able to speak freely with the Comanche and most other prairie tribes. Marcy said that Black Beaver was particularly good at identifying Indians' abandoned camps by the way their fires were built, and their lodges or tents constructed. Lieutenant A.W. Whipple used Black Beaver as he scouted for a railway between Fort Smith and Los Angeles in 1853 and 1854, and remarked that he "never forget a place that he had seen, even if many years had passed." If horses strayed, Black Beaver could find them.

Black Beaver's language skills came in handy. According to Thomas Foreman's 1946 *Chronicles of Oklahoma*, Marcy was visited by Comanche Chief Is-sa-ki-ep, who brought along the gift of two wives for the American leader. Marcy instructed Black Beaver to tell the Comanche that Americans have only one wife at a time. Black Beaver reported this astonished reply, "He say, Captain, you the strangest man he ever see; every man he seen before, when he been travlin' long time, the fust thing he want, wife."

It's worth pointing out that the broken English in quotes like this contrasts sharply with the highly articulate English letters Black Beaver penned. Whether this is because writers of the period invariably rendered Native speakers in pidgin or because Black Beaver's written prose was cleaned up by a collaborator, it's hard to say. In some cases, the same quote is reported by two sources with vastly different commands of the white man's tongue.

Black Beaver was overheard explaining to a Comanche guide that the whites believed the earth was round. He then described steam engines, and how they propelled huge boats up rivers. The Comanche was skeptical, claiming that his grandfather had actually been to the end of the earth and seen the sun set there. Besides, anyone could see that the prairie was flat. All this was outlandish enough, but when it came to the telegraph, Beaver refused to translate. "For the truth is," he said, "I don't believe it myself."

Black Beaver knew that the whites had loud voices, but couldn't accept that they could sit down to dinner then send the menu to a friend twenty days' journey away.

After Kiowas murdered Lieutenant Montgomery Pike Harrison (a grandson of President William Henry Harrison and a brother to President Benjamin Harrison) in 1849, Black Beaver was able to reconstruct the crime scene like a Native American Sherlock Holmes. He correctly sketched out the entire scenario, including the number of men at the scene, the animals they rode, and how the murder played out.

The aforementioned Major Israel Vore was a great friend of Black Beaver's and, according to *A Standard History of Oklahoma* by Joseph Thoburn, the two of them would stay up until midnight, night after night, as Black Beaver told the story of his life and Vore took notes for a possible book. Unfortunately, though the notes survived Vore's death, most were later burned. It's a pity, because an autobiography of Black Beaver would make enthralling reading.

Admiration for Black Beaver's ability rarely translated into the deserved recompense. And worse was coming. Soon after the outbreak of the Civil War, his by-then considerable property (worth an estimated twenty-five thousand dollars) was destroyed by Confederate troops while he was away serving as a guide to the Union Army.

The local Indian agent reported that Black Beaver then had "a pretty good double log house, with two shed rooms in the rear, a porch in front and two fireplaces, and a field of 41.5 acres [36.5 under cultivation] enclosed with a good stake-and-rider fence." He also had a good job as a translator.

Black Beaver's contribution to the Union cause was considerable. In 1861, he warned Major William H. Emory of approaching Confederate troops. Emory later said that Black Beaver "gave me the information by which I was enabled to capture the enemy's advance guard, the first prisoners captured in the war." The experienced scout—the only Indian who "would consent to guide the column"—then led Emory and his captured troops (a party of six hundred, delivered without any losses) to Fort Leavenworth in Kansas.

The path Black Beaver took was near where the Chisholm Trail (a major thoroughfare after the Civil War for driving cattle from Texas to the railheads) would later run through the southern border of Kansas. Paul Bennett, writing at Blackbeaver.info, says that the Indian scout may well have known Jesse Chisholm, since their careers "were parallel in time, geography and endeavor." They were born the same year. Some claim Black Beaver was with Chisholm when he died at Left Half Springs in 1868.

Hauptman writes, "Throughout the war, both Confederate and Union dispatches indicate Black Beaver's continuing role as a valuable Union scout." His work was well-known, and made him a marked man.

Black Beaver in scouting days. (Wikipedia)

The scout's farm was destroyed and his horses and cattle seized while he was away guiding the Union troops. This same fate awaited many other Delawares, the targets of bushwhackers who set fire to their cabins. The infamous raider William C. Quantrill operated in the Delawares' territory.

At the end of the Civil War, the Interior Department recommended removing the Delaware from their lands in Kansas and co-locating them in the Cherokee Nation. According to the Smithsonian's *American Indian* magazine, "Tribal leaders reluctantly

A BRIEF HISTORY OF BROKEN TREATIES

Here are a few highlights of just the early treaties with eastern tribes, courtesy of the collaborative Digital History:

In 1785, the US and the Cherokee Nation signed the Treaty of Hopewell, which leads to the total federal acquisition of the tribe's land. The 1791 Holston Treaty further eroded Cherokee claims. The 1803 purchase of the Louisiana Territory encouraged President Thomas Jefferson's relocation of eastern tribes west of the Mississippi River.

Between 1805 and 1833, the state of Georgia held eight lotteries to redistribute land taken from the Cherokees and Creeks. The 1814 Battle of Horse Shoe Bend, led by General Andrew Jackson, defeated the Creeks and led to a seizure of more than twenty-one million acres—from both friendly and hostile factions.

In 1825, President Monroe told Congress that all Indians should be relocated west of the Mississippi. The discovery of gold on Cherokee land was one motivator. The 1830 Indian Removal Act authorized the federal government to pay for the resettlement of eastern tribes. Alexis de Tocqueville witnessed the Choctaw removal in 1831, and described "the wounded, the sick, newborn babies, and the old men on the point of death . . . I saw them embark to cross the great river, and the sight will never fade from my memory."

The Trail of Tears continued. The Seminoles resisted evacuation, but their leader Osceola was captured and jailed, and the orders were carried out. The US Army invaded the Cherokee nation in 1838. The Cherokees were forced to march eight hundred miles to the Oklahoma Territory, and an estimated four to five thousand died.

The Homestead Act of 1862 opened up Kansas and Nebraska to white settlers. In 1868, Indians were denied the right to vote as part of the 14th Amendment, and control of the Indian agencies was handed out to twelve Christian denominations instead of army control.

According to Danna R. Jackson's *Eighty Years of Indian Voting*, Native Americans won the right to vote with the 1870 15th Amendment, but that wasn't the victory it at first appeared. "Despite their US citizenship and accompanying right to vote, historically Indians were prevented from participating in elections," Jackson wrote. "Indians were treated in a similar fashion to disenfranchised blacks in the pre-Civil Rights Act South."

Elizabeth Brown Stephens in 1903. A Cherokee, she walked the Trail of Tears in 1837. (Wikipedia)

agreed to sell all of their lands . . . Kansas and Washington politicians, traders and railroad officials profited greatly from the deal. Included in the profiteering was John C. Frémont, the Delawares' 'friend,' who was now a railroad magnate."

Marcy's journals describe Black Beaver as "a meager-looking man of middle size, and his long black hair framed in a face that was clever, but which wore a melancholy expression of sickness and sorrow." That, of course, was later in life, after experience had worn him down.

In an 1870 deposition, Black Beaver said that he'd been promised two thousand dollars for interpreting work, but only received $650. In 1872, when he was sixty-four and by his testimony too feeble to work for a living, Black Beaver filed a claim for damage of more than twenty thousand dollars (a fortune at the time) to his property on the Washita River by Confederate troops in 1861. He said he'd been promised compensation by Major Emory, and his claim was meticulously itemized. There was 250 head of cows and calves at twelve dollars each (three thousand dollars total), two hundred steers and heifers at ten dollars each (two thousand dollars), and much more, down to a two-horse wagon for $150 and a walnut table for five dollars. The total was $22,263.

The Indian affairs committee recommended only five thousand dollars, and it seems unlikely that Black Beaver ever received any of it. According to Hauptman, "In the late 1880s, his daughter, Lucy Pruner, was still writing in vain to the government, trying to collect the monetary damages promised to her father more than 25 years before."

This rough treatment didn't deter Black Beaver. In 1870, he attended the International Indian Conference in Okmulgee, Oklahoma and was a strong voice against raids by the plains tribes on whites in Texas. Two years later, he joined with Captain Henry Alvord and a delegation of plains Indians on a peace-making trip to Washington and New York, and was even reported to have had a private meeting with President Ulysses S.

Grant. As a former guide to the celebrated Audubon, he was met with acclaim at the Grand Central Hotel in New York.

The *New York Herald* reported, "The Red Men are on a tour to learn Fraternity and Christian Virtues." But by that time Black Beaver may have learned all he needed to about such virtue.

As late as 1878, Black Beaver was still acting as an interpreter for councils held at Okmulgee, and visited the Kiowa-Comanche Agency in 1874 to try and stop raids on Quaker communities. "The Quakers are your friends," he said. Despite his travails, Black Beaver was baptized at seventy and became a Baptist minister in his latter days.

In 1874, Baptist minister John McIntosh (born a Cree) hired Black Beaver to assist in missionary work. He reported, "On Sunday morning . . . Indians came with their guns, human scalps hanging to their belts as trophies, faces smeared with war paint. . . . Squaws dressed in gaudy blankets, and little or nothing else except the blankets, held crying babies." With Black Beaver at his side, "I opened the *Bible* and said to them, 'This is the word of the Great Spirit above to all his children,' and waited for Black Beaver to interpret it in their language."

Despite failing to gain compensation, by 1879 Black Beaver had once again become a prosperous citizen, and was reported to own three hundred acres, fully cultivated, with a large stock of hogs, cattle, and horses. And to his last breath (he died of heart disease in 1880) pushed for peace between the Indian tribes and white settlers. His old friend Vore offered a fine testimonial, noting the many generals and agents of the US government he served, "none of whom ever charged him with falsehood, or a dishonorable act."

WHAT HE SAID

Speaking to the International Council in 1872, held to promote peace among the tribes, Black Beaver said in part,

> Now I am an old man. I know all these people, my red brethren. I have traveled all over this country but I have never been over the waters . . . all this western country I know it, and it knows me . . . I have had pretty hard troubles, sometimes I see hard times, but I would not give up. . . . [T]he young chiefs are all here to . . . keep the war hatchet buried. We all want peace among ourselves and with the United States. . . . I hope we are united together, all chiefs—that's what we want, peace.

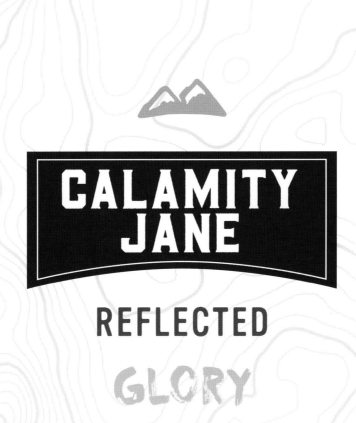

REFLECTED

GLORY

MARTHA CANARY ("CALAMITY JANE")

THE LEGEND

Calamity Jane was a muleskinner, stagecoach driver, Pony Express rider "over one of the roughest trails in the Black Hills country," and an intimate of both Wild Bill Hickok and General George Armstrong Custer. She was a lover of the former, and the latter benefited from her scouting prowess in Arizona circa 1870.

By her own account in the 1897 pamphlet *Life and Adventures of Calamity Jane*, the Custer trip was eventful. "During that time I had a great many adventures with the Indians, for as a scout I had a great many dangerous missions to perform, and while I was in many close places always succeeded in getting away safely." Why? Because she "was considered the most reckless and daring rider and one of the best shots in the western country." Some Indian observers thought she had supernatural powers.

Women didn't generally do these kinds of things, so to make them more comfortable Calamity started dressing up as a man. "When I joined Custer, I donned the uniform of a soldier," she said. "It was a bit awkward [but] . . . I soon got to be perfectly at home in men's clothes."

Calamity Jane got her name after the daring 1872 rescue of one Captain James Egan, commander of the fort at Goose Creek in Wyoming, who was shot by Indians and nearly fell off his horse. Jane caught Egan as he was falling and carried him back to the fort. On recovering, Egan exclaimed, "You are a good person to have around in a time of calamity. And I now christen you Calamity Jane, heroine of the plains." The name stuck. "I have borne that name up to the present time," Jane said.

In 1876, Calamity was traveling by stagecoach from Deadwood to Wild Birch in the Black Hills country when an Indian attack left driver Jack McCall wounded and incapacitated. According to *Progressive Men of the State of Wyoming*, "Although the other six passengers were men, none would take the reins. Jane mounted the driver's seat safely and in good time to Wild Birch."

Calamity Jane as General Crook's scout.
(Library of Congress)

The Jack McCall whose life Calamity Jane saved later murdered her paramour, Wild Bill Hickok. *Progressive Men* takes up the story.

> Calamity Jane was in the lead of the lynching party, and it was she who captured the desperado. She had left her rifle at home, but with a butcher's cleaver she held him up, and a very few minutes later McCall's body was swinging from a cottonwood tree and his soul had passed to the great divide. All old timers cherish her memory, as well they may.

The legend of Calamity Jane continues, and she has been portrayed many times on film and television by such actresses as Doris Day, Ellen Barkin, Anjelica Houston, Jean Arthur, Francis Farmer, Jane Russell, Yvonne de Carlo, Jane Alexander, and (most recently, in the TV show *Deadwood*) Robin Weigert. Day's energetic portrayal, which has her saying such lines as, "C'mon, you red-skinned heathens, come and get your one-way ticket to the happy hunting ground!" was perhaps the most popular.

The glamorization of Calamity Jane is all rather funny, because the contemporary *Black Hills Daily Times* once said she looked like the "a cross between the gable end of a fire proof and a Sioux Indian."

The earliest Calamity Jane picture, the silent 1915 *In the Days of '75 and '76*, is the first to depict a romance (and a marriage) between Wild Bill Hickok and Calamity Jane, but hardly the last. And because she sometimes dressed in men's clothing, Calamity is also something of a lesbian icon. Doris Day singing "Secret Love" in the film *Calamity Jane* is cited for its venting of forbidden feelings in the documentary *The Celluloid Closet*.

HOW THEY GET IT WRONG

Virtually nothing of what Calamity Jane (likely born Martha Canary) claims in her short autobiography is true, nor are many of the legends that grew up around her. The real Calamity Jane was trouble, a drunk, an illiterate, and a teller of tall tales who caused mayhem wherever she went—and that's the real origin of her name.

Calamity Jane with rifle. She used it to shoot up bars. (Library of Congress)

She didn't ride with the Pony Express, nor with Custer, didn't rescue Captain Egan, and the story about her personally avenging Hickok is romantic nonsense. The pair did meet, but Hickok thought she was obnoxious, and had only very limited dealings with her. (They *are* buried next to each other, though.) The vaunted ability with firearms was often employed to shoot up saloons, and far from being honored by her presence, many communities offered her one-way passage to the city limits (or threw her in jail until she sobered up).

Calamity Jane wasn't completely without accomplishments, but her legend was created mostly by dime novelists. Those ink-stained wretches—and later "biographers"—so obscured the actual facts of her life that it's difficult to form an accurate picture. What we can say is that Jane had an uncanny ability (James Beckwourth shared it) to be where western history was being made. And that made it easy for her to place herself at the center of events when she was really at the periphery.

Calamity Jane circa 1880. (Wikipedia)

WHAT WE ACTUALLY KNOW

Although there are many different birthdates extant (from 1844 to 1860) and different birthplaces, too, we now know through official records that Martha Canary (or Marthy Cannary Burk as she is in her pamphlet) was born in 1856, in Princeton, Missouri. In her accounting, her parents, Robert and Charlotte Canary, were originally from Ohio. And she was the eldest child in a family that included two brothers and three sisters.

That her family was from the Buckeye State is confirmed by census records, but she gives her own birthdate, incorrectly, as 1852. All the misinformation about her life is repeated in many biographies, which—in the absence of much other written material—use the scant, ghostwritten autobiography as a prime source. That's unfortunate but understandable, because there's no correspondence or many first-person accounts.

According to *Calamity Jane: The Woman and the Legend* by J. D. McLaird, "Most popular accounts make Calamity Jane a gun-toting heroine, claiming she was an associate of Wild Bill Hickok and served as a frontier scout, stagecoach driver, and Pony Express rider. Conversely, most scholars debunk her purported legendary achievements and depict her as little more than a drunken prostitute."

One of the latter is historian J. Leonard Jennewein, who opined, "With Calamity Jane we have the problem of the hero who performed no heroic deeds." That may be a bit harsh, but it's the basic dilemma. Rebecca Hein's online biography for the Wyoming State Historical Society asks the same question as McLaird—which Calamity is the real one?—and concludes, "The truth probably lies somewhere in between." She didn't do anything great, but she was a kind-hearted person with an ebullient spirit, and a special focus on helping people who were sick or injured.

Of course, it's the rootin', tootin' Calamity Jane who captured the public's heart and is depicted in countless films, books, and stories. Would Doris Day have played a drunken lady of the night?

As a child, Calamity says she enjoyed riding horses and "outdoor exercise." When her parents took the family—probably in search of gold—to Virginia City, Montana, in 1865, Calamity—already reportedly a crack shot at age nine—claims to have hunted with the men.

The census places a thirteen-year-old Calamity in Carter (now Sweetwater) County, Wyoming Territory, in line with her own account. She was orphaned by 1867, and McLaird says there's not much on the record to document what she did for the next five years—the period that's critical for establishing her legend.

Calamity says she went to Fort Bridger in the Wyoming Territory, arriving in May of 1868, then went to Piedmont, Wyoming, with the Union Pacific Railway. In 1870, she "joined General Custer as a scout at Fort Russell, Wyoming, in 1870, and started for Arizona for the Indian Campaign."

What is documented in a contemporary account is that in 1875, when she was nineteen, Calamity went into the southern Black hills with geologists Walter P. Jenney and Henry Newton to look for gold. A surgeon on the expedition, J. K. Lane, wrote an

*653 Calamity Jane

Copyright 1901 by C.D. Arnold

article for the *Chicago Daily Tribune* that included the line, "Calam
is dressed in a suit of soldier's blue and straddles a mule equal to any
professional blacksnake swinger in the army."

It also appears that in 1876 the young Calamity accompanied
General George Crook on a military campaign against the Sioux
and Cheyenne. But an eyewitness, Captain Jack Crawford, denies
she was ever a scout, and says Crook "gave her no recognition
whatever, except to order her out of camp when he discovered she
was a camp follower."

Nor does the tenure with General Custer—in 1870 or in 1874, as
she also sometimes claimed—stand up. Historian Dan L. Thrapp
says, "In her purported autobiography she claimed she scouted for

*Calamity Jane on horseback,
a fairly pitiful attraction.
(Library of Congress)*

the Army between 1870 and 1876, but there is no record that she was a scout. She said she went to Arizona in this capacity with Custer, but Custer never was in Arizona, nor was Jane at this time." She said she met Custer at a fort that wasn't even built when the general died.

There are no military records confirming she was paid as a scout, and she was never a prospector, either. Instead, she likely haunted the mining, construction, and military camps, working on and off as a prostitute—which is, after all, what "camp follower" meant in those days. Calamity Jane was definitely one of the first white women in the Black Hills, though. "She was a popular dance hall girl, bartendress and probably a prostitute," said McLaird in a TV documentary about Calamity Jane. He added that she was also a serious alcoholic.

Did she really rescue Captain James Egan, who then gallantly named her "Calamity Jane"? No chance. Egan denied the story, and so did his wife, and there's no record of the soldier being wounded at that time. Anyway, Calamity Jane gave other reasons for the nickname. She sometimes claimed it was Wild Bill himself who bestowed it on her, because of an uncanny ability to warn him of approaching enemies.

One biographer, Lewis Crawford, said it was her alleged work with smallpox victims that won her the new moniker. In 1901, the *St. Paul Dispatch* said she got the name because of "a faculty she has had of producing a ruction at any time and place and on short notice."

Perhaps the most credible story of how she became Calamity Jane comes to us via the *Washington Post* in 1906. The newspaper quotes George Hoshier, a friend of hers since 1875 who was also a pallbearer at her funeral.

> She was always getting into trouble," he said. "If she hired a team from a livery stable, she was sure to have a smash-up and have to pay damages when she got back. Why, if she'd got up to a fence rail, the durned thing would get up and buck. Calamity followed here everywhere, and so [James] Poulton [city editor of the *Cheyenne Daily Sun*] one day dubbed her 'Calamity Jane,' and the name stuck.

Calamity claimed to have ridden the Pony Express the fifty miles between Deadwood and Custer.

"It was considered the most dangerous route in the Hills," the autobiography says, "but as my reputation as a rider and quick shot was well known, I was molested very little, for the toll gatherers looked on me as being a good fellow, and they knew that I never missed my mark. I made the round trip every two days which was considered pretty good riding in that country."

Did she actually ride with the Pony Express? Feminist historian Kirstin Olsen argues, "She was rumored to have been a muleskinner, a Pony Express rider, and a stagecoach driver, although she was probably only the first." Many are the claims to have ridden with this short-lived but undoubtedly romantic mail service, and most are false.

In a 2005 *True West* magazine article, McLaird makes plain that many of the more outlandish claims failed to check out in public documents.

> The Calamity Jane that emerged from these records contrasted with the woman described in popular stories," he wrote. "Instead of wearing men's clothing and being a stage driver, Pony Express rider or gunfighter, Martha mostly wore a dress and worked in occupations expected of 19th-century women: laundress, waitress, dance hall girl and prostitute. Except for trips as a camp follower with military expeditions in 1875–1876, her buckskin outfit evidently was worn only during stage presentations and saloon performances.

In 1876, Calamity Jane met Wild Bill Hickok, and further burnished her reputation. According to Hein's account, she rode into Deadwood, Dakota Territory, that June with Wild Bill "in a conspicuous parade down the main street of the town. This episode began her rise to national fame." Calamity refers to "my friend, Wild Bill" in the autobiography, but there's no evidence that the two were close friends, and they certainly never married or became engaged, as she claimed.

A report with some credence from an eyewitness named Joseph Anderson indicates that Calamity got drunk, disorderly, and half-clothed at Fort Laramie as Hickok's party was arriving on the way for some gold hunting, and the soldiers begged the famous lawman to take Calamity (then in the post guardhouse) off their hands, offering up a buckskin suit for decency's sake. Thus it was that Calamity came to march through Deadwood, in frontier garb, with Wild Bill Hickok. Appearances were deceiving, because they barely knew each other, and that same year of 1876 Wild Bill was married to Agnes Thatcher Lake, the part-owner of a circus.

Almost everything Calamity said about Hickok was untrue, including her claim to have rescued his killer, McCall, from Indians then, after the murder, held the murderer at bay with a meat cleaver. In the autobiography, she even incorrectly identifies the saloon where Hickok held the "deadman's hand" of aces and eights, and was shot—it was Saloon Number 10, not the Bella Union. The consensus is that McCall fell off his getaway horse because the saddle wasn't properly cinched, then was captured by a large crowd of enraged citizenry.

At the end of the first season of HBO's *Deadwood*, Hickok's cowardly murder is depicted, and McCall is indeed captured by the crowd after failing to mount his horse.

Calamity Jane at Wild Bill Hickok's grave in the 1890s. (Wikipedia)

But the show's creators evidently wanted to split the difference between fact and fiction, because Calamity—while not linked romantically with Hickok—is still shown as better acquainted with him than she actually was.

In a 1902 interview, Calamity Jane made her most outrageous claim—that she and Hickok were engaged at the time of his unfortunate card game. At other times, she said that she and Hickok had been secretly married. She even asserted it was her actions that got McCall indicted, and later hanged.

Calamity did get married, in 1888, to the abusive William Steers, and they had a daughter, Jessie, born in 1887 (and deposited in a convent in 1895). She also spent time with, and sometimes claimed to be married to, Clinton Burke, and it's his name (spelled "Burk") that's on her grave and her autobiography.

Beginning in 1877, Calamity Jane (complete with glamorous gun-totin' portrait) was the heroine of Edward Wheeler's dime novels about Deadwood Dick, including one subtitled "Calamity Jane: The Heroine of Whoop-Up."

Standing erect on the back of her unsaddled horse, "her hair flowing wildly from beneath the brim of her slouch hat," Calamity races off to stop the destruction of the Whoop-Up mine. Sample prose: "She's a brick, Sandy . . . and just let et pop right inter yer noodle that she ain't no fool. She's a daredevil, Sandy . . . the most reckless buckaroo in these hills."

Wheeler, who described Calamity as possessing "a breast of alabaster purity," a "faultless waist" and "dainty feet," had never been west of Pennsylvania, but read stories about a frontier gal with a great name. His imagination did the rest.

A half-dozen such novels depicted Calamity Jane, and she became internationally famous. Meanwhile, the real woman was occupying barstools in the Dakota Territory from 1878 to 1881, and then the Montana Territory until late in 1884. She got more famous, and also drunker, and took to trading photos of herself for booze. Later, after 1897, she peddled her autobiography. Most of the Calamity Jane accounts from the Wyoming papers focus on drunk and disorderly charges against her.

Calamity Jane saw her fortunes improve with the rise of the Wild West shows. Suddenly, the stories she had peddled in saloons were in demand in dime museums, and she traveled to Chicago and beyond, even to Yellowstone Park to hit up the tourists. She went on the aforementioned tour with Liver-Eating Johnston.

"People poured in to see Calamity Jane," McLaird said. Kohl & Middleton advertised her in Minneapolis as "the famous woman scout of the Wild West!" and "the comrade of Buffalo Bill and Wild Bill!" It cost just a dime to get in to see this terror of evildoers in the Black Hills.

In 1901, Calamity traveled east all the way to Buffalo, New York, having been lured to the Pan-American Exposition by the somewhat mysterious and New York–based Josephine Brake—who exploited the frontiers woman's fame as a way of

Calamity Jane in show clothes. (Wikipedia)

promoting her novel. Brake tried to keep Calamity away from booze so she'd put on a good show, but it didn't work. According to the *Buffalo News*, Calamity was arrested there that August, "reeling from side to side." Always ready for a tall tale, she told the police it was her first arrest.

Calamity was paraded through the streets of Buffalo between the Apache Geronimo and Winona, a Sioux sharpshooter. But she was homesick, and claimed Brake (reportedly pocketing twenty-five dollars a week in exhibition fees) was "coining money at her expense," paying only meal money and proceeds from sales of the novel. Calamity told reporters that if need be she'd "adopt the role of a hobo" and ride the rails home to the west. It proved unnecessary, as Buffalo Bill Cody—who was visiting the exhibition—bought her a ticket home.

ANNIE OAKLEY: A REPUTATION EARNED

Despite not actually being a westerner (she was born and died in Ohio), Annie Oakley (original name: Phoebe Ann Moses) was everything Calamity Jane wasn't. She was a crack shot, and that was enough—she never pretended to have killed Indians, trapped furs, or scouted for military campaigns. She was steady, reliable as a veteran performer, and charming. She was devoted to her husband, Frank Butler, an Irish-born marksman, and they were together until her death in 1926.

When her father died and the family fell on hard times, eight-year-old Oakley went out and shot a squirrel with the rifle that hung over the fireplace. By 1875, when she was fifteen, Oakley was supplying local shopkeepers with game and made enough money to pay off the mortgage on the family farm. She entered a shooting contest that same year, and that's where she met—and beat—Butler. He lost the match but won the girl.

By 1882 the couple were regulars on the vaudeville circuit. In 1884, Oakley's audience in St. Paul included Sitting Bull, who was entranced by the sight of Oakley shooting out the wick of a candle. He gave her the Indian name "Watanya Cicilla," which stuck in translated form as "Little Sure Shot." In 1885, Sitting Bull and Oakley were reunited as members of Buffalo Bill Cody's Wild West show. She was a top star there for most of the next seventeen years.

Among other tricks, Oakley would shoot the ash of a cigarette in Butler's mouth (in Europe, she did this trick with Kaiser Wilhelm II), hit the edge of a playing card from thirty paces, repeatedly shoot and shatter tossed glass balls, and hit bull's-eye targets while looking in a mirror. Audiences never got tired of her, and she never let them down.

Oakley's reputation was unimpeachable, and that's why she filed multiple claims—and won all of them—when William Randolph Hearst's scandal sheets reported in 1903 that she was in jail for "stealing the trousers of a negro in order to get money with which to buy cocaine." If you substitute "whiskey" for "cocaine," you might get something Calamity Jane would do.

Oakley retired in 1913, and with Butler moved to a waterfront cottage in Maryland. She was much better off than her old friend Bill Cody, who'd gone bankrupt by then. Oakley volunteered to lead a women's sharpshooting battalion in World War I, and when that was turned down she gave shooting demonstrations to Europe-bound troops. She died in 1926, with Butler following soon after. Twenty years later, Irving Berlin's evergreen *Annie Get Your Gun* debuted, and she gets her man in that one, too.

Upper left: Annie Oakley by Baker's Art Gallery, circa 1880. (Wikipedia)

Lower left: Annie Oakley in later years. Still a sure shot. (Library of Congress)

Above: Annie Oakley was the real deal, but no Westerner. (Library of Congress)

FEMALE DESPERADOES: THE BANDIT QUEEN AND THE STAGE ROBBER

Pearl Hart is another western legend, and not for good reasons. She left her gambler husband and son in Canada, moved to Arizona, and, facing money woes, began a life of crime—initially robbing men she'd lured up to her room.

With a German drifter named Joe Boot as partner, hair cut and dressed like a man, the petite Hart—who looks proud of herself in all surviving photographs—robbed the stage running between Florence and Globe, Arizona, with drawn guns in 1899—taking $421. The amateurs left a trail a blind man could follow, and got lost during the getaway—they were quickly caught. At the trial, Hart famously said, "I shall not consent to be tried under a law in which my sex had no voice in making." Nevertheless, Boot got thirty years, Hart (after first being acquitted with a story about needing the money to visit her sick mother) five. She escaped once, got recaptured, and was paroled in 1902.

Hart later attempted to cash in on the vaudeville stage as "The Arizona Bandit," and some sources say she became a model citizen and settled down to a quiet and happy marriage. But the record shows she was arrested in 1924, charged with stealing canned goods.

Then there's the legendary "Bandit Queen" Belle Starr, who dressed in buckskins and a man's Stetson, and was always ready to draw her pistols. Starr (originally Myra Maybelle Shirley, born in 1848) started out respectable, having trained as a classical pianist in Missouri.

Starr met Cole Younger of the bank-robbing James-Younger gang in 1866, but the stories that she had a child by him are almost definitely not true. Instead, Starr married the shady Jim Reed, and had her first child by him. Reed was involved in whiskey smuggling, stage robbing and other crimes. Originally just married to an outlaw, Starr soon was one herself, perhaps as legend has it bedecked in velvet skirts and plumed men's hats, brandishing a pair of pistols and riding her horse, Venus.

Reed was killed by a member of his own gang in 1874, and Starr fled to Oklahoma Indian Territory—where she married and resumed her bad behavior with a Cherokee named Sam Starr, who was from a notorious criminal family. They were caught in 1883, but after a few months in jail for horse thefts they were at it again. Starr was well known for harboring criminals (possibly including Frank and Jesse James) on the Indian land, telling the *Dallas Morning News*, "I am a friend to any brave and gallant outlaw."

Theft wasn't a career with long-term prospects, especially at that time. Sam Starr was killed in a gunfight in 1886, and Belle found another Indian partner. In 1889, just before her forty-first birthday, the Bandit Queen was ambushed and shotgunned in the back while riding home to her ranch. There were numerous suspects, including her last Indian husband, a disgruntled tenant, her estranged son, Ed, and even her daughter Pearl. Nobody was convicted. That same year, the dime novel *Bella Starr: The Bandit Queen or The Female Jesse James* appeared. Its reliability is questionable.

"A more daringly eccentric woman I have never met," Cody said at the time. He also said Calamity was a "big-hearted woman, generous to a fault." That generosity, which may have included helping out a miner named Jack McCarthy, who'd broken his leg, is frequently cited as a saving grace.

Calamity was back in South Dakota by the fall of 1901, having taken a circuitous route because she kept drinking up the ticket money. There isn't much more to her story. The Wild West Calamity had known was gone, and the new version wasn't friendly to shooting up saloons. She posed for a picture at Wild Bill's grave, and wandered around from bar to bar.

Calamity's standard order was, "Give me a shot of booze and slop it over the brim." Calamity was certainly generous when it came to liquor—she'd borrow five dollars then buy everyone in the room a drink and be broke again. When generous townspeople paid

Above: Failed bandit Pearl Hart never could hide the smirk on her face. (Wikipedia)

Right: Belle Starr and "Blue Duck," circa 1886. (Wikipedia)

into a fund to educate her daughter, they made the mistake of giving her the money—she promptly drank it up.

Writer Lewis Freeman, who ran into Calamity in Livingston, Montana, that year, wrote in *Sunset* magazine that she "was about 55 years of age at this time and looked it. . . . Her deeply lined, scowling, suntanned face and the mouth with its missing teeth might have belonged to a hag of 70." She was actually forty-five. Despite appearances, Freeman described Calamity as "the sunniest of souls."

The sunny soul's financial plight had been publicized in the newspapers, and she received donations from Buffalo Bill Cody and others. She died in a hotel room in Terry, South Dakota, age forty-seven, in August of 1903. Her wish to be buried next to Wild Bill was honored, because the city fathers of Deadwood (who gave her a fancy funeral) saw that it would help them make a buck. Hickok would have objected, but he was dead. The gravestone initially said she was "Aged 53 Yrs."

In a bizarre footnote, a woman named Jean Hickok McCormick went on the popular "We the People" radio show in 1941 and claimed to be the daughter of the secretly married Calamity Jane and Wild Bill. She tenderly placed flowers on Wild Bill's grave and produced what she said was Calamity's "diary," but this fraudulent document, consisting of letters to the daughter who'd been given up for adoption, was in handwriting suspiciously similar to McCormick's own. Besides, the woman born Martha Canary was illiterate.

The McCormick material is collected in a beyond-unbelievable book called *Calamity Jane's Letters to Her Daughter*, and the author is given as one "Jane Cannary Hickok."

WHAT SHE SAID

From the autobiography, a typical burst of hyperbole: "I left Deadwood in the fall of 1877, and went to Bear Butte Creek with the Seventh Cavalry. During the fall and winter we built Fort Meade and the town of Sturgis. In 1878 I left the command and went to Rapid City and put in the year prospecting."

JOE KNOWLES

NATURE MAN

OR FABULOUS FAKE?

JOSEPH KNOWLES

THE LEGEND

He's no longer well-known, but Joseph Knowles was a superstar in the years surrounding World War I, when he was "The Nature Man." Before reality television was ubiquitous, Knowles was a pioneer. In 1913, he went naked into the Maine wilderness, carrying nothing (not even a knife) and emerged victorious two months later, clad in the skin of a bear he'd caught in a makeshift trap.

Knowles's adventures were covered daily in the sponsoring *Boston Post*, complete with his charcoal illustrations, and the wilderness hero's return to the city was met with a gala parade, cheering throngs, a leaf-strewn gala dinner at the new Copley Plaza Hotel, and the key to the city from John F. Kennedy's grandfather.

The Nature Man was a Maine native, and his wilderness skills were honed as a northern hunting and fishing guide. At the publicity-hungry *Post*, locked in a tight circulation war, he was the staff artist who regaled his colleagues with tales of his prowess in the woods. So why not send him out and see what happened?

Joe Knowles wrote a bestselling book about his exploits, *Alone in the Wilderness*, and toured successfully for $1,200 a week on the vaudeville circuit. So successful was his

Left: Joe Knowles heads into the woods of Maine. (From the autobiography)

Facing above: Joe Knowles disrobes. (From the autobiography)

Facing below: Elaine Hammerstein, a sensation until she declared she didn't want to kill animals. (Library of Congress)

Maine sojourn that the *Post*'s bitter rival—
the Hearst chain—hired him to repeat the
experiment in the remote California wilderness.
There, he had the attention of top scientists and
medical men who studied, documented, and
filmed his survival techniques.

The outbreak of World War I interrupted
what would have otherwise been a second gala
performance. But Hearst wasn't done with
Knowles—it sent him out once more, in 1917,
in the Adirondacks—this time with the science
spiced up with an Eve for his Adam.

A national contest was held to find an
appropriate wilderness maiden, and the unlikely
anointed was one Elaine Hammerstein, a
successful film actress and first cousin to
celebrated songwriter Oscar. She was certainly
beautiful enough to merit slavish press
attention, but her usual haunts were the wilds
of Manhattan and Beverly Hills.

Alas, the third expedition was aborted, and
Knowles headed for Hollywood, where he
(having already made a documentary focusing
on his wilderness skills) starred as the lead in a
western potboiler. He even wrote a screenplay.

By then, Knowles was an icon for the Boy
Scouts of America, which republished his
book and took him on as a Scout Leader in the
Pacific Northwest. Knowles flourished there

Above: Joe Knowles during his brief Hollywood period. He appeared in a documentary about wilderness life, starred in a potboiler western, and wrote an unpublished semi-autobiographical screenplay. (Wikipedia)

Below: The crowd comes out to see Knowles arrive in Boston. (From the autobiography)

as a regional artist, painting official portraits for the governors of two states and decorating movie theaters and hotels with his Remington-inspired paintings of sailing boats and the winning of the West. He ended his days in a makeshift beachside cottage (built out of driftwood) on the rough Washington coast near the mouth of the Columbia River.

Why did Knowles strike such a chord with the public? Why did they pay good money to see him on stage building a fire by rubbing sticks together? After all, in 1913 most people—even the city dwellers—had grown up on farms and presumably had some wilderness skills. But the supposedly unsinkable *Titanic* had just gone down (in 1912), and there was concern about a rapidly mechanizing and urbanizing world. There was general anxiety that the rural life was disappearing.

Wilderness themes are prominent in other popular literature of the period, such as Jack London's 1903 *The Call of the Wild* and Edgar Rice Burroughs's 1912 *Tarzan of the Apes*. Knowles went into the woods at the right time. Given TV shows like *Naked Castaway*, *Dating Naked*, and *Naked and Afraid*, it looks like we're in a similar historical moment today.

HOW THEY GET IT WRONG

Joe Knowles was always a controversial figure, and some of that mystery remains to this day. Did he really survive unaided in the wilderness for two months, or did he hole up fully clothed in a remote cabin, subsiding on canned beans brought in by Maine guides of his acquaintance? It's still not clear.

Joe Knowles is examined. The doctors were astounded at this physical specimen. (From the autobiography)

Knowles's effect on the *Post*'s circulation (he doubled it) did not go unnoticed by the newspaper's rivals. Hearst's *Boston Sunday American* bided its time then struck a devastating blow with a November 30, 1913, exposé, "The Truth About Knowles: The Real Story of His 'Primitive Man' Adventures in the Maine Woods." It claimed he'd been living cozily with his unnamed manager in a log cabin near Spencer Lake, and even received regular visits from a mysterious woman friend.

The story, supposedly based on a seven-week investigation, claimed Knowles actually bought his (bullet-ridden) bearskin from a local trapper for twelve dollars. Knowles's bear trap was so shallow that "a cat could have hopped out of it with ease," the exposé said. It even went so far as to assert that Knowles's illustrations—supposedly written on birch bark with charred sticks from his fires—showed evidence of pencil lead.

Knowles was enraged, and certainly didn't act the guilty man. He came speedily back from the lecture circuit and staged a spirited defense replete with threats of a libel suit. Boston was riveted, and a major newspaper war erupted. The *American* initially retreated, canceling the story in later editions. But then it changed its mind and defended its work.

Knowles makes fire. He repeated this trick many times for paying audiences. (From the autobiography)

Much revolved around that bearskin. Knowles, who was still wearing it on public appearances, stoutly denied it was full of bullet holes, and offered to show it to any comers. A friend of Knowles did indeed pay twelve dollars for a skin, but that was a *different* bear. "There are plenty of them there to shoot," the Nature Man said. Knowles went so far as to stage a somewhat campy exhibition of his bear-trapping-and-skinning skills. A poor ursine was brought to Knowles's original bear pit, whereupon Knowles clubbed it to death and dressed the skin in front of witnesses.

Knowles fought his rivals to a standstill in 1913, and emerged with his reputation only moderately tarnished. He was still alive in 1938, when the *New Yorker* published a bemused "Where Are They Now?" piece on The Nature Man that named one Michael McKeogh as the manager who had helped Knowles in the Maine woods.

McKeogh claimed he actually wrote Knowles's diary entries on a typewriter in that remote cabin, and that Knowles was a lazy collaborator who had to be coerced to dig his bear pit. The bearskin? Indeed purchased for twelve dollars. The big-city story has a major weakness—aside from the questionable veracity of some of its sources, the author made no attempt to contact Knowles, who was then very much alive.

The *New Yorker* did not print letters to the editor at the time, so Knowles's response to being slandered was printed in the local *Chinook Observer* instead. He wrote, "If the charges were less ridiculous, the article might have been more convincing. From the back-stage of 1913 appears the ghost of McKeogh with a fantastic tale defaming Knowles. What a break for the writer."

Later accounts do cast some doubt on Knowles's two months in Maine—including an eyewitness's 1973 claim to have seen a newly built cabin on the shores of a Nature Man haunt, Lost Pond. Behind it, said Helon Taylor (a boy in 1913, but later superintendent of Baxter State Park) was "a pile of beer bottles and tin cans about four feet high." Taylor later recanted and said he believed "every word" of Knowles's story.

In 2013, two relatives of Maine guide Allie "Tripe" Deming (hated by Knowles) surfaced to say that Deming claimed the Nature Man had matches and food on his trip into the wild. Also, that Knowles had asked Deming to scratch his body up with blackberry bushes to make him look more authentically weathered.

But for every report like this there are others swearing that Joe Knowles was legitimate.

NAKED IN THE WOODS

Joe Knowles was such a hit in the woods that he inspired many Adam and Eve imitators, most of whom came to grief.

A group known as the "Six Eves" offered to go naked into the woods (under Knowles's supervision) in 1916. A couple named Carl and Margaret Sutter, backed by the *Boston Advertiser*, took a Knowles-like plunge into the trees and got themselves arrested by game wardens near Ashland, Maine, in 1922. They were supposed to stay six weeks, but made it through two. It wasn't just the law: Maine is seriously buggy in the summer, and Eve got badly bitten.

Even in the mid-1930s, the Joe Knowles effect was still powerful. The *Portland Sunday Telegram* sent the Maine-bred Bradley brothers, Arnold and Kenneth, naked into the woods at Maine's Moosehead Lake. They did better than most, succeeding in creating fire, gathering food, and creating a neat lean-to. But then a snowstorm blew through, deposited seven inches of powder, and the experiment was over after thirteen days.

WHAT WE ACTUALLY KNOW

Joe Knowles probably was faking it in the Maine woods, despite his undisputed wilderness skills. It seems likely, though, that his second trip into nature, in California in 1914, was legitimate. For one thing, Knowles was in territory unknown to him, without accomplices. Secondly, he was closely watched by a scientific delegation that included Thomas Talbot Waterman of the University of California at Berkeley anthropology department, a star player in the deification of Ishi, the so-called last wild Indian in California. Ishi was set up as an exhibit at the university's anthropology museum, and gave bow-and-arrow demonstrations for Sunday visitors.

Ishi and Knowles appeared on a San Francisco stage together (the former in a suit, the latter in his bearskin). Waterman jumped at the chance to study Knowles. The Nature Man's methods "will be watched and compared to the methods of primitive peoples," Waterman said. "He should open up a fund of wood lore that will be of interest to scientists as well as the average man who loves the woods . . ." Knowles himself opined, "I suppose they call Ishi a faker, too."

The tone of Knowles's early California dispatches are quite different from the jaunty notes in Maine. He sounds both depressed and hungry. "I have done nothing so far but exist," he wrote about his fourth day. Although his spirits later picked up somewhat, it's unclear how the expedition would have ended had not the Great War erupted that August. The world conflagration pushed Knowles off the front pages, much to his chagrin.

Waterman, who observed Knowles as often as he could, remained a true believer. But few people were watching at that point. According to the *American Mercury* in 1936, "It was a hell of a note for Joe Knowles. The Naked Thoreau news went into the back pages next to the classified ads, and many a Californian doesn't know to this day if Knowles *ever* got out of the woods."

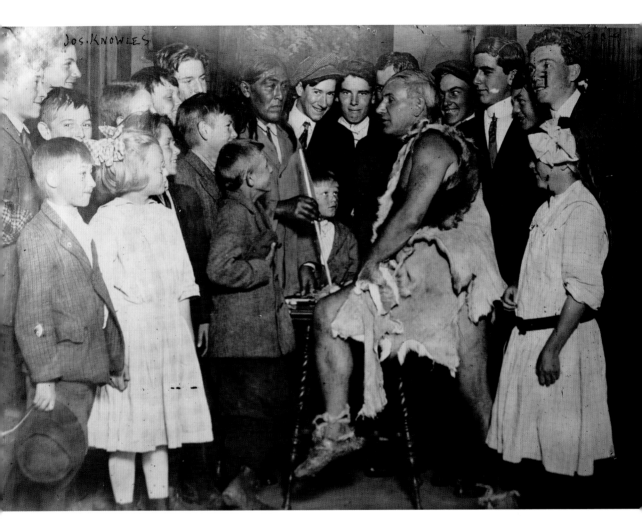

Knowles in his bearskin, Ishi in a suit, surrounded by young admirers at their joint San Francisco appearance. (Library of Congress)

Ishi, known as the last wild Indian in California.
(Library of Congress)

A thorough examination of Knowles's papers, which are held at Ilwaco Heritage Museum and other collections in lower Washington, makes a few things clear. He had a rather lofty self-regard, but was no writer—and *Alone in the Wilderness* was almost certainly ghostwritten by a newspaper accomplice. His papers contain numerous drafts of an autobiography, and invariably they start strong, wander off on tangents, and then end abruptly.

Was Joe Knowles a nature faker? Yes and no. He held an authentic store of wilderness knowledge, and knew that wolves don't come to the aid of stranded campers. He *could* have conquered the Maine woods legitimately, but he was lazy.

In his Pacific cabin, Knowles was happy enough, though he dreamed of recapturing the attention he had briefly enjoyed as the Nature Man.

WHAT HE SAID

In one of his early birchbark missives from the Maine woods in 1913, Knowles wrote, "My object is not to show how many wild creatures I can destroy, but rather how few I will need to supply me with the absolute necessities of life and comfort." He said that the birds and animals "are my friends and neighbors."

INSPIRED BY JOE KNOWLES

The exploits of Joe Knowles inspired the prolific T. Coraghessan Boyle to adapt his story for the 2000 novel *A Friend of the Earth*. Set in the future California of 2025, the book features Knowles's great-granddaughter Andrea, who repeats her ancestor's experiment with her eco-conscious husband in tow.

Amazingly, they make it through a month in the woods, but not without being eaten alive by every bug in the woods. The insects double as dinner—along with salamanders and earthworms.

For his book *Under the Stars*, a history of camping, Dan White was inspired both by Joe Knowles and my 2007 biography of him. In 2013, he went naked into the Soquel Demonstration State Forest in the Santa Cruz Mountains of California's Central Coast—exactly one hundred years after Knowles.

"It felt so freeing to be naked in a place like this," White wrote. "I couldn't remember the last time I was that present inside my body." It started out well. He felt one with the earth ("for the first time I really *smelled* the forest"), but then the yellow jackets descended, stinging him seven times. He survived an uncomfortable night, stings throbbing, but concludes, "At least I was uncomfortably alive."

ACKNOWLEDGMENTS

First of all, I'd like to thank Keith Wallman for coming up with the idea for this book. To him I owe the splendid time I had writing and researching it. And I'd like to thank Michelle Branson of Gibbs Smith for ably carrying the manuscript along to completion.

I also commend the noble souls of Archive.org for not only providing such a thorough inventory of the Grateful Dead's live concerts, but also a huge cache of just about everything else, including full-text versions of just about all the early mountain man biographies and autobiographies.

The historical societies of several states, including Wyoming, Oklahoma, Montana, and Missouri, deserve mention for maintaining important archives, and keeping the interest up with important, well-researched articles. Similarly worth kudos are the gifted amateurs who operate sites such as Beckwourth.org, HughGlass.org, JohnLiverEatingJohnston.com, and AmazingWomenInHistory.com for their research—and posting of original documents.

Similarly, I applaud the many online researchers who posted original documents and essays on the mountain men, and the authors who wrote fascinating books about them—including Louis S. Warren, Richard Slotkin, Hampton Sides, and many more.

Thanks to Nathan E. Bender of the Albany County Public Library in Laramie, Wyoming, for his insights and editorial help with the chapter on "Liver-Eating" Johnston. Thanks also to the other Nathan E. Bender, who took my call with good humor when I was trying to find the historian.

I'm indebted to Kerry Holton, president of the Delaware Nation, for his insights into the life and career of the admirable Black Beaver.

I commend the many scholars and interested parties who got in touch after I published *Naked in the Woods*, to which this book is something of a sequel. I appreciate the dialogue, and I hope it happens with *The Real Dirt on Americ's Frontier Legends* as well.

Thanks to my wife, Mary Ann, for ceding me the lion's share of the standing desk, where most of this was written. And my kids, Maya and Delia, by being amused—up to a point—by my stories about people like "Liver-Eating" Johnston.

BIBLIOGRAPHY

Abbott, John S. C. *Daniel Boone: Pioneer of Kentucky*. New York: Dodd & Mead, 1872.

Allen, Michael R. *Western Rivermen, 1763–1861: Ohio and Mississippi Boatmen and the Myth of the Alligator Horse*. Baton Rouge: Louisiana State University Press, 1994.

Averill, Charles. *Kit Carson: Prince of the Gold Hunters*. Boston: G. H. Williams, 1849.

Bakeless, John. *Daniel Boone: Master of the Wilderness*. New York: William Morrow & Co., 1939.

Blair, Walter, and Meine, Franklin. *Half Horse Half Alligator: The Growth of the Mike Fink Legend*. Chicago: University of Chicago Press, 1956.

Bonner, T. D. *The Life and Adventures of James P. Beckwourth, Mountaineer, Scout, Pioneer and Chief of the Crow Nation of Indians*. New York: MacMillan and Company, 1892.

Burns, Ken and Duncan, Dayton. *Lewis & Clark: The Journey of the Corps of Discovery*. New York: Alfred A. Knopf, 1997.

Cody, W. F. *Story of the Wild West and Camp-fire Chats*. Philadelphia: Standard Publishing Company, 1888.

Crockett, David. *A Narrative of the Life of David Crockett of the State of Tennessee*. E. L. Carey and A. Hart, 1834.

Derr, Mark. *The Frontiersman: The Real Life and the Many Legends of Davy Crockett*. William Morrow and Company, 1993.

The Editors of American Heritage. *The American Heritage History of the Great West*. New York: American Heritage Publishing, 1965.

Faragher, John Mack. *Daniel Boone: The Life and Legend of an American Pioneer*. New York: Owl/Holt, 1993.

Filson, John. *Discovery, Settlement and Present State of Kentucke*. London: J. Stockdale, 1784.

Glasrud, Bruce A. *Buffalo Soldiers in the West: A Black Soldiers Anthology*. College Station, Texas: Texas A&M University Press, 2007.

Gregson, Susan R. *James Beckwourth: Mountaineer, Scout and Pioneer*. North Mankato, Minnesota: Capstone/Compass Point Books, 2006.

Grossman, James R., editor. *The Frontier in American Culture*. Berkeley: University of California Press, 1994.

Hauptman, Laurence M. *Between Two Fires: American Indians in the Civil War*. New York: Free Press, 1995.

Hurd, Owen J. *After the Fact: The Surprising Fates of American History's Heroes, Villains, and Supporting Characters*. New York: Perigree/Penguin, 2012.

Josephy, Alvin M., ed. *Lewis and Clark Through Indian Eyes*. New York: Alfred A. Knopf, 2006.

McLaird, James, D. *Calamity Jane: The Woman and the Legend*. Norman, Oklahoma: University of Oklahoma Press, 2012,

McMurtry, Larry. *Oh What a Slaughter*. New York: Simon & Schuster, 2005.

Morgan, Robert. *Lions of the West: Heroes and Villains of the Western Expansion*. New York: Workman/Shannon Ravenel Books, 2012.

Motavalli, Jim. *Naked in the Woods: Joseph Knowles and the Legacy of Frontier Fakery*. Cambridge: Da Capo Press, 2007.

No author listed, *Story of the Wild West and Campfire Chats*. Philadelphia: Historical Publishing Company, 1888.

Peters, Dewitt. *The Life and Adventures of Kit Carson . . . from Facts Narrated by Himself*. Hartford, Connecticut: Dustin, Gilman & Company, 1874.

Progressive Men of the State of Wyoming. Chicago: A. W. Bowen and Company, 1903.

Remini, Robert V. *Andrew Jackson: The Course of an American Empire*. Baltimore: Johns Hopkins University Press, 1998.

Rochlin, Fred and Harriet. *Pioneer Jews: A New Life in the Far West*. New York: Mariner Books, 2000.

Russell, Don. *The Wild West: A History of the Wild West Shows*. Fort Worth, Amon Carter Museum of Western Art, 1970.

Scott, Hugh Lenox. *Sign Talker: Hugh Lenox Scott Remembers Indian Country*. Norman, Oklahoma: University of Oklahoma Press, 2016.

Sides, Hampton. *Blood and Thunder: An Epic of the American West*. New York: Doubleday, 2006.

Slotkin, Richard. *Gunfighter Nation: The Myth of the Frontier in Twentieth-Century America*. New York: Atheneum, 1992.

Smith, Richard Penn, and Crockett, Davy. *Col. Crockett's Exploits and Adventures in Texas*. New York: William H. Graham, 1836.

Stegner, Page. *Winning the Wild West: The Epic Saga of the American Frontier, 1800–1899*. New York: The Free Press, 2002.

Thoburn, Joseph Bradfield. *A Standard History of Oklahoma: An Authentic Narrative of Its Development, Volume 1*. Chicago, New York: The American Historical Society, 1916.

Thorp, Raymond W., and Bunker, Robert. *Crow Killer: The Saga of Liver-Eating Johnson*. Bloomington, Indiana: Indiana University Press, 2016.

Tucker, Phillip Thomas. *Exodus From the Alamo: The Anatomy of the Last Stand Myth*. Havertown, Pennsylvania: Casemate. 2011.

Wakeman, Sarah Rosetta. *An Uncommon Soldier: The Civil War Letters of Sarah Rosetta Wakeman*. New York: Oxford University Press, 1996.

Wallis, Michael. *The Real Wild West: The 101 Ranch and the Creation of the American West*. New York: St. Martin's Press, 1999.

Warren, Louis S. *Buffalo Bill's America: William Cody and the Wild West Show*. New York: Alfred A. Knopf, 2005.

Wood-Clark, Sarah. *Beautiful Daring Western Girls: Women of the Wild West Shows*. Cody, Wyoming, 1983; rpt. 1992.

Wright, Mike. *What They Didn't Teach You About the Wild West*. Novato, California: Presidio, 2000.

INDEX

JIM MOTAVALLI writes for the *New York Times*, The Wharton School at the University of Pennsylvania, *Barron's*, NPR's *Car Talk*, Autoblog, *Natural Awakenings*, and others. He lectures frequently on environmental topics in the US and abroad. Motavalli is a two-time winner of the Global Media Award from the Population Institute, and hosts a radio program on WPKN-FM in Connecticut, with frequent guests and live music. He lives in Fairfield, Connecticut.

ALSO BY JIM MOTAVALLI

High Voltage: The Fast Track to Plug in the Auto Industry

Naked in the Woods: Joseph Knowles and the History of Frontier Fakery

EarthTalk: Expert Answers to Everyday Questions about the Environment

Green Living: The E Magazine *Handbook for Living Lightly on the Earth*

Feeling the Heat: Dispatches from the Frontlines of Climate Change

Breaking Gridlock: Moving Toward Transportation That Works

Forward Drive: The Race to Build the Clean Car of the Future